NEW WRITING / BOOK TALK / NE

THE REA

GW00360275

No. 63 AUTUMN 2016

Published by The Reader

The
Reader

CONNECT
REALISE
CHANGE

EDITOR   Philip Davis

DEPUTY EDITOR   Sarah Coley
CO-EDITORS   Marjorie Lotfi Gill
                        Angela Macmillan
                        Fiona Magee
                        Brian Nellist

ADDRESS   The Reader Magazine,
                        The Reader,
                        Calderstones Mansion House,
                        Calderstones Park,
                        Liverpool,
                        L18 3JB

EMAIL   magazine@thereader.org.uk
WEBSITE   www.thereader.org.uk
BLOG   www.thereaderonline.co.uk

DISTRIBUTION   See p. 127

COVER   Artwork 'Therapy' by Joe Magee

ISBN 978-0-9935610-2-3

SUBMISSIONS

The Reader genuinely welcomes submissions of previously unpublished poetry, fiction, essays, readings and thought. We publish professional writers and absolute beginners. Send your manuscript with SAE please to:

The Reader, Magazine Submissions, Calderstones Mansion House, Calderstones Park, Liverpool, L18 3JB

Printed and bound in the European Union by Bell and Bain Ltd, Glasgow

NEWS AND EVENTS

ANYTIME IS STORYTIME

In August over 600 children and carers enjoyed stories for free on Anytime Is Storytime day as part of the Liverpool City of Readers campaign. Building on last year's success, we doubled the scale of the project and developed a strong relationship with Give A Book, who managed to negotiate for us fantastic bulk donations from Walker Books, Pan Macmillan and Penguin Random House. Thirty-eight staff and volunteers from local and national organisations including The Reader, Beanstalk and Merseytravel helped us deliver storytelling in 13 locations across Liverpool.

POETS DON'T LIE

August also saw the launch of The Reader's new anthology *Poets Don't Lie: The Reader Volunteer Anthology*. Volunteers from across The Reader were invited to submit favourite poems to this anthology with submissions coming from those working on many of our projects, including Big Lottery Merseyside and Wales, Leicester, Barnet in London, and the Off the Page project in Liverpool. These recommendations represent the personal and real connection that our volunteers have with literature, as well as being a record of the generous act of engaging with older readers through reading, talking and sharing thoughts. Copies are available for £6 on The Reader website: **www.thereader.org.uk**

LOOKED AFTER CHILDREN IN EDUCATION

In June our patron Lemn Sissay spoke to school governors and educators gathered for the Looked After and Learning conference at Liverpool Hope University. Drawing on his own experience in care – such as having breakfast for the first time with a new foster family – Lemn talked about the resilience of looked-after children, the demands their circumstances place on them and the skills they use on a daily basis, just to achieve a level of normality in their lives. He ended with a call for schools and teachers to raise their aspirations for looked-after children and look at each individual beneath the label.

CONTENTS

ANYTIME IS STORYTIME

See p.3

6

FLIGHTS AND PERCHINGS

Philip Davis

There are some thoughts you don't know what to do with. So sometimes I have been putting them down here, in so-called editorials. Forgive me, but here is one.

Some years ago I was having trouble with my eyes. I remember standing at a Merseyrail station after an appointment with a consultant and thinking about the genuine possibility of something closer than ever to blindness. It may have been sheer shock but I found myself thinking a thought that also felt rather calm.

It was this sort of feeling. That if I could avoid talking about it to anyone, if somehow I could keep what was happening and going to happen inside me and away from social sympathies, then perhaps it could just become a part of my story, something natural that had happened that I would then go on living with. This was implausible: I had concerned and loving people I would have to tell and even rely upon later, and it is doubtful I could have held off the physical reality coming down on me like a blackout, whatever I tried to think inside.

Still, this attempt at acceptance, if that is what it is supposed to be called, wasn't at all normal for me. It is not that I am a 'Why Me?' type. I think almost anything could happen to almost anyone, accidentally, without right of complaint. 'Why Not Me?'

is my badge of preference, for better and worse. But usually I cannot believe that It (whatever it is, as it is happening) is wholly and ineluctably real, cannot think that this is something I won't get away with this time, but will be permanent. That's maybe because I have thought of a lot of things that could happen, and they haven't, and the very capacity to imagine or anticipate reality then makes reality itself uncertain. Sometimes, knowing I could think or talk myself into anything, I have wanted to ask someone close: what do you think is going on? You know the joke about the two psychoanalysts meeting in the street, and one immediately says to the other, in greeting: 'How am I?' That's my question. I have said this before: when people routinely ask me how I am doing, not meaning much by it after all, I have had to learn to stop myself saying, honestly, 'I don't know'. They don't like that answer.

But as you get older, of course you wonder: when some terrible definite and nonnegotiable prognosis is delivered, as there are good chances it must be at some time, then how will I react or manage? How am I, doc?

Now, however, I am thinking of the other possibility. That something that might seem Terrible - according to quite reasonable social conventions, and in line with future apprehensions inevitably taken from outside the situation as it will turn out to be – that supposedly Terrible thing, I say, might not have to be as it seems, if only one could keep one's individual nerve and view it from the inside, more instantly, more microscopically. I think I mean this: that too often we go along with the slow, big, known names – This is a Disaster, This is Something-That-Should-Not-Have-Happened, or even This is How-It-Should-Be. But actually inside, and for the split-seconds of truly real life and action, whatever it is is not to do with past vocabularies. It is to do with a present that is surging into a future (not The Future, but the very next excited micro-second) which it does not wholly know. When you do know, it's gone. By truly real action here, I mean quick moments when you instinctively decide to say something or do something, or some decisive thought occurs, or an opening or opportunity or calling suddenly beckons, with excited liveliness in place of old routine. Then it feels very intimate and interior, a disposition kept both prior to naming and beyond past stereotypes, in involuntary imagination of something you may be about to get to. When you get to it, it may become unexcited and familiar again: I managed

8

to say the right word to a friend; I suddenly saw what might be done; I realized something I had not before. I am saying we live most and best in an almost immediate future, not the past. And that immediate future is the present, if we called it aright.

I fear this may not quite make sense. You may want more specifics, some examples, and I am not sure I can give them when what I am describing is an interim experience, a sort of loophole within reality that is abstract with potential not yet realized and perhaps never fully realizable. But here is my favourite William James again on transitions – that strange nameless place between A and B that I suggest is oddly more important than perhaps either of them:

> **Like a bird's life, consciousness seems to be made of an alternation of flights and perchings. The rhythm of language expresses this, where every thought is expressed in a sentence, and every sentence closed by a period. The resting-places are usually occupied by sensorial imaginations of some sort, whose peculiarity is that they can be held before the mind for an indefinite time, and contemplated without changing; the places of flight are filled with thoughts of relations, static or dynamic, that for the most part obtain between the matters contemplated in the periods of contemplative rest.**

It is that very temporary resting-place in between the sentences, silently driven from behind whilst still looking to go forward, which is to me an image of what I need to keep hold of inside, in the midst of life and between the acts. It feels more like a hint than a solution. But if I could sustain this 'attitude', as I find myself wanting to call it, I might somehow be all right, I think.

This might of course be nonsense, or worse, hubris.

ineluctably: against which it is useless to struggle

EDITOR'S PICKS

We have new poetry from **Bibhu Padhi**, **Gareth Culshaw**, **David Constantine**, **Stuart Pickford** and **Vincent Parker**. In Poet on Her Work, **Jane Bonnyman** talks about her poem 'Ferns' which reflects her lifelong fascination with Robert Louis Stevenson and his wife, Frances Matilda Van de Grift.

Jennie Feldman's story 'Flight' is a story about friendship, and the differences between seeing at distance and in close up. The Old Story comes this time from **Rudyard Kipling**, 'The Miracle of Purun Bhagat'.

Nick Benefield, psychotherapist and policy maker, talks to Fiona Magee about his work in prisons and his lifelong interest in the human individual: 'We've no right under criminal law to deprive prisoners of anything other than their liberty. What an institutional environment such as a prison does a lot of the time is it squashes the capacity for human interaction.'

Conor McCormack, filmmaker, writer and psychoanalyst writes about his documentary film *In the Real* which follows people who hear voices: 'I've always been drawn to making films about people who are on the outside of things.' **Kim Devereux** (*Rembrandt's Mirror*) writes about female role-models presented in the media and women's internalised struggle to resist those images: 'I believe that nothing short of changing the very way we look at bodies can stop this madness. What we need is Rembrandt's eyes.'

Please do continue to send us your selections for our One-Pagers. We love to know what you are reading and thinking. This time passages from **Thomas Hardy**, **Shakespeare**, **Nye Bevan** and **Joseph Conrad**.

OUR ADDRESS

Submissions and correspondence to be sent to Calderstones Mansion House, Calderstones Park, Liverpool, L18 3JB.

July 2021

FICTION

FLIGHT

Jennie Feldman

Still no sign of them. She straightened, blinking hard against the wind. They must have dived and come up somewhere else, invisible in that grey expanse. Again she peered through the lens. Even without the elusive birds, the close-up held her gaze: sinewy ridges veined with foam. She could have been looking over the side of a ferry.

'Any luck?' His voice, not yet familiar, made her start. 'Devil-divers, they're called. Hard to keep track of them.' Taking her place at the telescope, he swivelled it round towards the shallow lagoons inland. 'Ah, but no missing these!' He adjusted the focus. '*Tadorna tadorna*. Take a look.' The lens held a striking portrait: bright red bill, black head and neck, a neat body patterned in white, black and chestnut.

The shelduck was one of his favourites, he had said the day before, showing her the entry in his bird guide; another – the page dog-eared for easy reference – was the delicately camouflaged

snipe with its long, thin bill. 'Two ways of taking in the world:
one rakes the surface, the other probes in the mud.' As they talked
and sipped drinks, the book lying open on the table where she
had joined him ('Weren't you on the sea path this morning?'),
uncertainties of depth and surface had lent a peculiar pleasure to
the afternoon. He taught Classics at a public school nearby. 'Or
rather,' he quickly corrected himself, 'I used to teach – until last
year.' In the autumn he had gone on a week-long hike in Cyprus.
He paused and took a long draught of beer. One day, he said
quietly, he had come across a mist net strung between trees. It was
swaying and jerking, five small songbirds trying to free themselves.
He looked at her and shook his head, 'Just unbelievable.' By the
end his fingers were stained red and he was shaking from head to
foot. Another pause. 'They all got away,' he said. But their bony
softness as he held them, hacking at the net with a penknife – that
had stayed with him. Gave him a new connection with birds…
She nodded, waiting. Beside them the log fire spat and settled.
Then he had glanced up, trying to smile. 'How about yourself?'

The wind off the sea had suddenly gathered force and with
it came ragged veils of drizzle that blew across the low dyke, its
narrow path tracing the coastline into the distance. Time to pack
up the telescope. Since they were going opposite ways – he lived in
town, she was staying at a bed-and-breakfast in the other direction
– they agreed to meet at the same spot the next day. The forecast
was brighter.

As she peeled off her damp socks she caught sight of the envelope
– had she forgotten she'd tossed it there? – lying unopened on the
bed, the writing depressingly familiar. She dried her hair and made
a cup of tea, stirring it lengthily. Finally she picked up the letter
and opened it. *…found this forwarding address and am hoping you're
still there. Why the away message on your email? Listen, if you fly
off…* By now it was raining in earnest, the view from the window
blanked by furious lashings on the glass. Wearily she crumpled the
page, then smoothed it flat on the bedspread, absently stroking
out the wrinkles with her palm. An old habit took over, folding the
paper in half, turning down the corner flaps, folding up the base.
When the boat hatched into shape, she set it on the sill where it
wobbled in the draught from the darkening storm outside.

There was no one in sight next morning when she reached
their meeting place. Perhaps she had got it wrong? But there was

the flat patch, now waterlogged, where he had set up the tripod. He must have been delayed. She sat on a rock and waited, the morning sun warm on her back, the air lazy with chirrups and rustlings and hoarse repeated cries. Then a more human sound. It was him, walking briskly towards her, almost running. Her wave went unanswered. 'Come!' he shouted. His face was strange with anguish. 'Please,' he panted as he reached her, 'Come!' He seized her hand and turned back.

Even at that distance, twenty or thirty yards, there was no mistaking the chestnut band across the white breast. The bird's bill lay vivid against the mud, its webbed feet useless in the air. She gazed sadly at the dead shelduck. 'So sorry,' she whispered. But he seemed not to hear. He buried his face in his hands and dropped to his knees, sobbing uncontrollably. Then she was crouching beside him in the damp grass, an arm around his shoulders, noticing for the first time a greying at his temples. His grief – that was the only word for it, she thought, bewildered – expended itself slowly.

Slowly, over the next few days, he unpacked his life. It lay in heaps around them like discarded clothes. By the door his walking boots stayed put. One early morning she slipped out alone, this time following the sea path further than usual to where it swerved inland and the nature reserve ended; at its entry gate a placard told visitors this was once the site of a centuries-old salt industry. Behind the dykes these lagoons had served as drying pools. Docks and channels had been carved out for barges bringing coal to evaporation pans. Please respect the wildlife, keep dogs under control.

For a while she stared at the illustrations in disbelief. Gouged and slashed, exploited on an industrial scale – this same teeming, forgetful haven! She turned and began to walk back. Did he know, she wondered, the history of the place? Almost certainly. She thought of him sitting at his desk, looking up from his reading. Greek and Latin texts had become vital again, propped open as he made notes. And she saw the little boy cradling his lifeless canary, his father threatening to wring his neck too if he didn't stop his bawling. She had nearly reached their old meeting place on the path. Somewhere the trilling of a curlew hung on the air. Time will do it, she thought. Now that there is understanding. How else does one go about greening a ravaged childhood?

Sperat infestis, metuit secundis... The woman sitting next to her was eyeing her quizzically. She must have spoken the words aloud.

Gazing out on the clouds she repeated them to herself softly. The marvel of their compactness. In the book he had given her, a small pencilled tick marked favourite passages. 'Be hopeful in trouble / Be worried when things go well'. He knew passages from the Odes by heart, in Latin and English. Gifted out of thin air, it seemed. Now Horace, tucked in beside the Instructions in Case of Emergency, would carry his voice. *I feel the feathers softly gather…* Clouds were thinning, islands below, specks of boats. That line – wasn't it from the final ode in Book Two, the one he had ticked twice? She flipped to the page: '*I feel the feathers softly gather upon / My shoulders and my arms, becoming wings. // Melodious bird I'll fly above the moaning / Bosporus, more glorious than Icarus // I'll coast along…*'

31st August 2020

BIBHU PADHI

A Way To Pray
On An April Morning

Watch your mind.
The thoughts –
they always rush in.

Stay where you are. You will
hear the almost-zero sound
that stays on with you.

Not the sound
of the old bus gurgling
out its own smoke;

not the sound
of mosquitoes crackling
against a killer-net.

Nor the sound of summer
in the ceiling fan's cool,
miraculous recovery

of your life to yourself;
nor the rare bird's whistle
among banana plants.

Nor the illegible sound
of your own breath
through the body's chemistry.

No. Another sound.
Accompanying you wherever
you go, turning with your turns,

enveloping you as if in a
circle, expanding, including
all that you are, you are not –

your dreams, illogical
thoughts, the rumours
that always travel with you,

your days and nights,
ever-shifting thoughts.
Like Creation,

a discovery. Stay in it;
watch your thoughts.
And then close your

eyes and see how empty
the mind is, as if
it was not there, ever.

2nd July 2022

Choices

When it comes to choosing
from more than one pain,
tears emerge from secret places,
the belief in oneself is eroded
by the smallest differences.
They all seem to come from
the same place, carrying similar
lonelinesses. The mind and heart
suffer attacks of an elaborate grief
that is beyond all choosing,
all available rules of choice
and exclusion. The tears
come forth again, against
your wish, even as you feel
weak and alone, while the world
moves on its ancient road
of forgetting all that is close
to you, including those
much-diffused tears of a while ago.
Alien eyes suspect the story behind
your residual tears, even as you
turn away, remember –
more than ever before – your
own stories of loss and insult,
how you were excluded in story
after story by someone else's
grief over choices
and the consequent pain of loss.

OBSCURE LIVES

The Mayor of Casterbridge by Thomas Hardy is dominated by Michael Henchard. There are two mayors of Casterbridge, of course, but Donald Farfrae leaps into no reader's mind. Henchard's temper and his force of life seem to overshadow everyone, especially his colourless wife Susan.

Susan dies of a wasting illness and the townspeople (Hardy's 'extras') gather in the street to gossip about Christopher Coney who is rumoured to have dug up and spent the pennies Susan had prepared for her eyes:

> **'Well, poor soul; she's helpless to hinder that or anything now,' answered Mother Cuxsom. 'And all her shining keys will be took from her, and her cupboards opened; and little things a' didn't wish seen, anybody will see; and her wishes and ways will all be as nothing!'**

What I love about this passage is that the speaker is of no consequence in the book; the event is awful in its mundanity (pennies stolen to spend on beer); Susan herself hardly ever seemed to register as a character, and yet Mother Cuxsom's eulogy has the effect of throwing a light onto the reality of someone's particular life. 'Her wishes and ways will all be as nothing!' It's a delicate lament and yet Susan's wishes and ways gather in that moment of thought. It's a curious ghostlike moment.

Michael Henchard's nihilistic last will is famous: 'That Elizabeth-Jane Farfrae be not told of my death, or made to grieve on account of me. / & that I be not bury'd in consecrated ground / & that no sexton be asked to toll the bell [...] & that no man remember me. To his I put my name' but who dare say how much or how little real feeling and thought lie behind Mother Cuxsom's words on Susan Henchard.

WHILST NOT FALLING APART

Fiona Magee talks to Nick Benefield

Interview with Nick Benefield – Psychotherapist and policy maker. Nick was Department of Health Personality Disorder Advisor and Joint DoH/NOMS (National Offender Management Service) Offender PD Programme Head. Recently retired, he lives with his wife, Jen, in Cheshire.

What's your connection with The Reader?

I first found out about The Reader around 2006, when I met Jane (Davis, founder of The Reader) and we talked about how Shared Reading might fit into the idea of how you engage people through methods other than traditional therapy. Along with colleagues, we are responsible for establishing in criminal justice settings the environmental model of living, management and care known as PIPES – which stands for Psychologically Informed Planned Environments. Reading groups were the first of what we call the 'enrichment projects' as part of this. I funded an initial piece of work with The Reader back in 2010 and they now run reading groups in every PIPE in the UK.

What's the thinking behind PIPES?

PIPES are established in both prisons and in criminal justice settings in the community. They are part of a pathway approach to the longer term care and management of high risk offenders. It is not sufficient to lock a person up and get them fed and watered, we need to create environments that support psychosocial life and character development, to further day-to-day stability and foster long-term hope. I think it is one of the most optimistic things happening in prisons at present.

It is a life programme and a long business. We track improvements in their social and psychological behaviours, their general psychological health, as well as ultimately a reduction in their risk of offending. Already we have some evidence that people are doing a lot better. We've only been at this now for five years, so only a few have come out so far, but of the ones who do come out the indicators are that they feel more stable and equipped to be back out in the world when they come to leave prison.

Why did you think Shared Reading would be a good fit?

My feeling is that people in these settings can get a new start in this area of experience by being read to. Reading is a very rewarding experience. If we think about what happens for children when they're being read to: they make sense of their environment and how they fit into that. In some way it builds a picture for them about how the world is and then they can actually marry it with the reality. We learn about good and bad, right and wrong kindness and unkindness – the whole range of emotions and many life scenarios. These ideas can be rehearsed and worked out – better understood without too much anxiety. Children (and later, adults) hear stories and they build up *internal narratives about how life is both for themselves and others.*

Internal narratives? Can you tell me more about that idea?

A man or a woman in a prison has done something very wrong that got them there and they have a story, an internal narrative, about their life – how they got to where they got to. Often it's things like, 'It's all because of my ex' or 'This happened to me when I was young' or sometimes, 'It wasn't me, it didn't really happen'. Those narratives are there, fundamentally, to preserve their sanity. If you've harmed someone you've got to have a narrative that makes it possible in some way to live with it. The alternative being that you become very defensive and bury it so it's untouched and you drop it away from consciousness.

What we need is men and women in this position to be able to gradually face that difficulty, to change the narrative about it, because their existing narrative is incorrect – it doesn't give them any responsibility ('my dad beat the living daylights out of me') or blames the victim. What you need is for them to have a more complex narrative that gives them an understanding that they both own a responsibility and aren't solely responsible. In other words some choices and decisions were driven by all sorts of other factors in their lives.

What sort of factors?

Most of the men and women in the offender PD (personality disorder) programme have chronically deprived, often traumatised and broken early years. I don't mean that's the *reason* they commit bad acts but I would say there's a direct relationship between early deprivations and traumas and later anti-social behaviour. If a child has a positive environment that is socially and relationally rich, that supports the neuropsychological development of the individual the brain to some degree. If the *opposite* happens, we now know that this tends to lead to a poorer quality of relating later, a poorer containment in the individual and poorer emotional management.

What do you mean by containment?

I mean holding onto yourself, being yourself, being able to relate to others whilst not falling apart yourself; I mean not being disruptive and being collaborative – so you can have friends and relationships, which of course go up and down but you can generally *manage*. I'm talking also about what we might call an internalised moral capacity and things like being assertive but at the same time still considering others. All of these things are subtle but very important latent social skills and a significant number of the prison population have not been given the experience to develop these skills. Around 34,000, at the last estimation, fit the criteria for having a severe personality disorder likely to be related to their criminal offending and are probably a risk to their self and particularly to other people. There's a lot of people who we don't help; prison provision might work as a deterrent for individuals who are relatively normal psychologically, but actually most of these men and women *aren't* as robust.

But there is help that can be given? Can you tell me more what form that takes?

My work is about trying to understand; if children get most of this ability to learn early by the way they're reared and attached and safe, what might we do with a man or a woman in their early thirties who's committed a serious crime and is in a prison? We can't regrow brains, but we *can* provide an experience which they can internalise – give them a good experience that they enjoy, feel valued in and respected by, that is social and some way equated to early childhood experience of attachment and safe relationships.

Over the years I've been to so many prisons and secure hospitals and I was disheartened by the poverty of those environments – low levels of support for improving relating, no art, no creative workshops – so little through which you might learn something new, afresh, that might feed you in some way and give you a sense of something other than the basic day-to-day provision. The Reader seemed to be ready-made for bringing a new level of ongoing psychosocial enrichment into those environments.

You're not talking here, are you, about teaching literacy, but something else?

If people want to learn to read and write, that's great but that must not be the purpose of why people are in the context of the Reader we are 'reading to' in a prison, although Mr Gove – Liz Truss now – might possibly disagree. To me, what the reading groups should be about is giving special time to these men and women without laying any expectation on them.

If you just stick with the idea of trying to teach people to read, it can become bound up with shame and failure – you can get to the literacy issues, but not until you've first overcome the discomfort, the anxiety, the inhibition, the early failure, all that sense of 'I stutter over words and I can't get them right, and yet I'm a 30-year-old man who was tough on the street'. These are things we know are very hard for people to overcome. To be read to is to be given a reading plus experience.

OK, so what is the value of this 'special time' they are getting in the reading group? What does it do?

I think there are a few things going on. Firstly, getting these men and women to read together in a group gives them a richer experience of *social* life and allows them to test out how to be orderly with one another too: Can I be relatively normal in a group of other people? Can I have my views challenged? Can I be listened to or listen and wait for other people to speak? All very simple social skills these people often have missed out on.

And secondly, it gives them a richer *interior* life. It allows people to rework experiences, to rework aspects of themselves, taking on other references and viewpoints. If I'm a man who has done harm, and I'm in a high secure prison my place in the world in one sense is a very rigid fixed point – this is who and what I am. I am a serious offender in prison – doing my time. All of the stuff we do on PIPES units, including the reading groups, allows for some *re-triangulation*: it allows the identity of the person to become a little bit more fluid and able to incorporate something else other than their fixed narrative – does that make sense?

Back to the idea of changing narratives?

Yes, because when you read, and particularly in a group, all the time you're hearing other people's views. What happens is you don't have to keep your old narrative going – you become less defensive and you can test out a new narrative, and the thing is you're doing it with the story – the story removes it slightly from you, so you don't have to expose yourself too far, you can put something out there and see what people make of it. You're growing your capacity to explore varying views on how life is, to test out various ideas and perspectives.

What you're essentially asking the people in the reading group to do, is to put themselves in somebody else's place. There is a brilliant book, *This is Water* by the philosopher David Foster-Wallace – we bought it for all the PIPE teams – and it's about how you've got to keep at the job of thinking, 'So what's happening on the other side, what's it like to be the other person?' Because if you don't, the danger is you only get to the division that says 'They are different than me and I don't like their difference' and that's that. Life is then only one-dimensional, my view alone.

I visited one of our reading groups in HMP Frankland recently, and the clinical lead there said to me: 'The men see the reading group as a break away from their treatment, but in fact it is part of their treatment'. Do you agree?

Yes! But we don't need them to see it as part of their treatment. However, we do need the prison or hostel to understand that it has a therapeutic potential. The other concern is that this is early days in a long term initiative and we have to be careful about how this sort of provision is perceived. It's only two years ago, remember, that there was a ban on books in prisons. All these enrichment activities – reading, singing and drama – they can be seen as in some way too pleasurable for offenders and so we might receive a negative press.

Because…not punitive enough?

Look, none of this is a science, but it's my feeling that when we put someone into prison, we need to maximise it as an opportunity – with reading, with singing, with any enrichment projects and good relating and good 'parenting' – if we want to turn those people into better citizens. We pay maybe £50,000 a year to put one man into prison. Why waste that? It must be seen as an investment.

We should treat our prisons as better places, as part of our world, and then *our* world would be better. I was recently visiting a prison in an Overseas Territory and it was a place where we would all agree conditions were shameful. And OK, compared to that, in our prisons we generally follow good human rights; the prisons themselves are generally clean and tidy, but actually the experience of being a human in a prison? If we were to go and live in a prison for a month or two, I think we would have a new perspective on how much the setting supports good human relating. We've no right under criminal law to deprive prisoners of anything other than their liberty. What an institutional environment such as a prison does a lot of the time is it squashes the capacity for human interaction. I understand that, to some extent it has to, for lots of very good reasons about safety and risk, but my principle is, if you treat people badly you get bad people (from babyhood onwards) and if you treat them as well and respectfully as possible, then you're generally going to get better, more responsive people. The trouble is, that like a lot of things, prisons are an industrial model for a human problem – and trying to change that is a hard balancing act. A good many prison Governors and staff work to reduce the worst impact but it's often an uphill struggle because the conditions work against it.

I'm interested in your emphasis on the 'human'. That's about, is it, compassion? But also imperfection?

The men and women we work with, they're real people with real difficulties and we can make a difference in the time we've got where we deprive them of their liberty – we can maximise the opportunity, in PIPE units at least, for supporting the improvement of human relating. We want people to be better related and better relaters. If we can't get on being in the presence of other people, you are more likely to be in trouble. Many of these men and women are deeply troubled by their relationship to others: personality disorder, which is what most of them have, is fundamentally a difficulty in the relationship between the person themselves and the world – 'this doesn't look right,' 'that person's not behaving properly' 'he shouldn't have said that' – everything, for them, is troubled and it's persistent, pervasive and problematic.

But not hopeless?

Donald Winnicott (paediatrician and psychoanalyst) said, 'The delinquent act is an act of hope'; in other words if I take, I take because I think I might one day have. Many people act that hope out through acts of physical taking, so stealing for example – many years ago we looked after a boy who used to steal and every time he stole he threw the money down the toilet, just flushed it all away, never kept or used it. It was the act of the taking that was the thing. I'm very moved by people in prisons sometimes – I'm quite hard-nosed in other ways because I know how harsh the world can be for people but I've met people in prison for whom I realise their resilience and their still holding onto something means… there is a hope for them, you know?

Would you call what you do a vocation?

No, it's a profession, but, you don't do this work – and lots of people do this work and do it better and in a more organised way than me – unless you feel that you can *do* something, fulfil some kind of purpose. I don't mean that in a pompous way, like, 'One must do good in the world', I just mean I love personhood. I'm not an idealiser of people, quite the opposite – there are lots of difficult bits about relationships in life and sometimes I think things can be dreadful! – but it's the stuff of life, isn't it? I couldn't *not* be interested in people.

Is that what led you into your career?

I'm not sure. I've never really planned a career – every five years something would seem to fall into place and be naturally the next thing to do. I was one of six brothers and sisters and we were brought up as Methodists – I left going to church when I was a teenager at fourteen. But, I think I identified early on in my life that in some way you're here for a purpose. My mum and dad were great believers in education; he was a trade unionist and he thought education was the way out of poverty, and they liked the arts – one of my brothers was a violinist, one an artist, others were nurses and teachers; we all did public sector jobs and I think my parents were proud of that.

I had quite a chequered history at school: I went to a Grammar school and I loved it there and did quite well until I got to exams and I failed rather badly. Despite this, the headmaster allowed me into the sixth form. Nowadays they wouldn't do that, but I think he knew I was probably bright enough but I was struggling with some things in growing up and so was worth the perserverance. However, I didn't finish sixth form, I dropped out – I think academically I was a bit crushed at the end of school when I left. My dad was very kind and said that I could leave school if I had a job.

And that first job was….?

I looked in the paper and I got a job as a housemaster at a boarding school in Surrey and I left home with a suitcase and a record player and I cried! I was an eighteen-year-old, paid to look after twelve to fourteen-year-olds and I knew nothing about looking after them. I had a decent model of what a caring, family set up was like, but this place was terrible, pure institution. I spent two years learning how *not* to look after children and thinking it was exactly what I *didn't* want to do with my life. I realised then how unpleasant life was in places that were institutionalised and how it was not the way to look after people.

How did you develop your ideas about what is the way to look after people?

Probably through the job I did next. After social work training I began working at a place near Cirencester called The Cotswolds Community, which was in the process of changing from being a children's prison into a therapeutic unit. I was a residential social worker and social therapist there for twelve years.

I was responsible for a lot of very difficult kids, in a place that had no locked doors, no punishments, eight staff, and we ran a small farm-holding, milked cows, kept sheep, baked bread, all that sort of thing. I enjoyed it; it was hands-on working with people and I learnt all about therapeutic social work and about Donald Winnicott's work of 'good enough' upbringing.

I still see some of those children – they're men with families of their own now. Most appear to have done well.

And the psychotherapy? How did that come about?

I started my own analysis and began training as a psychotherapist, moved to London and developed social group work in Islington and Family Service Units and eventually completed my psycho-therapy training.

I took on the Directorship of Hammersmith Mind in London and I worked there for eight years, then my wife Jen and I came up here to Cheshire, bought a derelict house and garden with two friends and had to find a job. I thought I'd have a go at NHS commissioning – ended up commissioning forensic services in the North West for Ashworth and all the medium and low secure services. I started a multidisciplinary team there which included a prison governor, a psychiatrist, a nurse, a psychologist, a social worker, a probation officer, so you had a more integrated team commissioning all of those services.

And the fact that it is a 'mixed team' is important?

Yes. The health service, in my view, lost the core task for psychology some years back when psychology services became more specialist and access more limited. In the context of the Offender Personality Disorder Programme I wanted psychologists to go and work on the floor in prisons with the officers, so they are fully present as the psychological mind in the prison setting. I wanted them freed up from doing just assessments and offender treatment programmes, to being able to make a difference to the day-to-day lives of people – spotting and getting people early, working with them, seeing it as a life-long plan and thinking about them all the way through out into the community: so it's more than just a psychological intervention.

What about the place of prison officers – how do they fit into this idea?

I once said to two prison officers who complained that each day started so badly with angry exchanges as men were unlocked at breakfast, 'When you go to unlock a prison door and take your key out of your fob, just for thirty seconds think about the man, the individual, behind that door. *Then* open the door'. I was back there a few weeks later and they said, 'You know you told us to do that thing about the keys, well we've started doing that and mornings are a lot better here now'.

It's a different way of working. I've met a lot of officers who've told me that they were miserable, they didn't want to come to work, but since they've been working in the PIPE setting that's all changed. They can't imagine why nobody ever told them this is what it could be like in a prison. They've started to feel they can treat prisoners thoughtfully, with more respect and as individuals – I hear prison officers talk to me about individual prisoners in a way that they never would have done years ago; they speak as though they're talking about real human beings who they understand have done bad things, they must look after them safely, but they have expectations and hope for them. That is a great gain. And it leads to more steady and stable prisoners because they feel cared about by the staff and related to.

If we could just get people to understand that prisons are depersonalised worlds in which humans are organised into institutional living that tends to replicate their life experiences in a negative fashion. We want prisons to be the opportunity to provide with emotionally reparative experiences. To make time in prison more live and human because these people don't get much experience of that and they're going to come out and live in the world again here they will need to be more emotionally and socially literate.

It's a big ask of everyone involved – the men and the officers – isn't it?

Yes, I suppose it is. The men in particular perhaps. We are asking them to trust; they have to trust and that can be hard. They come to the reading group and they have to watch the reader and the others in the group in order to think, 'Is this safe?' Just the listening, speaking and tolerating other people's response is so big an issue if you have had few opportunities to develop safe experiences of being with others. They're not asking a conscious question about safety but that's what's going on.

A lot of the men couldn't engage, they wouldn't start therapy and so we had to try and work out what happens when you are suddenly confronted with something unexpected in relating terms – like the reading group for example. Why might they find it hard to take up something that is offered and which, over time, might help. We wanted to understand and learn *what makes engagement safe*, what are the rules? So for a while I conducted a sort of informal experiment. I would strike up conversations with strangers and have a conversation for 3–4 minutes. I wanted to better understand what happens in this fearful, uncertain space of the first engagement with an unknown 'other'. I had some very interesting even startling experiences and saw how very different it was for the range of individuals I approached. I got on a Tube one day, it was full and I had to stand, and an elderly saffron monk offered me his seat. I said 'No that's fine' and he sat back down.

When a seat came up opposite him, I sat down and leant across and said to him, 'There are not many people in London that would offer a man of my age a seat' (I was in my late fifties) and he said, 'You looked tired'. Just a few words, but they cut across so much of the social norm. This simple attention to what you observe as to the state of the other person means you can make more responsive approaches that are tuned into where the other person may be at that moment. This level of attention can break through so that your approach is felt to be more in tune with the person and is adapted to 'fit' where they are and how they might be feeling.

This may sound very simple but it is surprising how little we are able to maintain that sort of attention, and for people who have had poor early experiences of sufficient attention to their emotional states it is very important.

I'm wondering about you as a reader. I see how it works in our Shared Reading groups but for you? When you pick up a book what are you after?

I want to know why we are as we are, I want to know more about us being us – the world, people, civilisation. A book has to give me something that adds to the colour of life. A good novel , poetry and non fiction that can all provides additional knowledge of another perspective about our being here in the world with all its joys and failings. It's the same as observing how we are with each other, how people are managing with both good and not so good life experiences. I can only live my own life but I can learn and benefit from attending to others.

Doing the work I have done and living my life the way I have is so closely entwined that I am lucky enough I rarely have to feel that work is anything other than being in life. It has had a great impact on my valuing of so many different experiences, and books can add a great deal to that understanding and enrichment of being here just now.

POETRY

GARETH CULSHAW

Door Latch

When we moved here things would be
different. From the twist and push or
lever down, push, there was a new way.

Gate sounding, heavy looking, feather light
it made you think that bit more before
entering. a pause on things.

Letting the feet slow down, time is now
thought of, as maturity comes with a tap
and slap of a door latch.

JANE BONNYMAN

© Gerry Cambridge

32

THE POET ON HER WORK

ON 'FERNS'

Jane Bonnyman

S ince I first encountered Robert Louis Stevenson at an early age, I have become intrigued not just by his captivating 'yarns' but also by the man himself: he comes across as an inspiring, creative and overall optimistic character, with a deft ability to rally against the odds; someone whom you'd definitely invite round for dinner and he'd be just as happy squatting by a campfire under the stars as in a chandelier-festooned dining room. Thus, inspired by Emily Ballou's 'The Darwin Poems', my original intention was to embark upon a biography in poems, drawing on research into Stevenson's own personality, adventures and extensive travel. But then I read about his wife.

Frances Matilda Van de Grift was born on 10 March 1840 in Indianapolis, Indiana. By the time she was twenty she was married to Samuel Osbourne and had had one daughter, Belle. Her husband proved unfaithful and she later divorced him to marry Robert Louis Stevenson after meeting him in France. Before her marriage to Stevenson, she had already travelled across America and to Europe and experienced life in the silver mines of Nevada surrounded by Indians; she also lost her youngest child, Hervey, after he died in Paris from tuberculosis – a tragedy that was to haunt her for the rest of her life. Not only was she an adventurer, she was also greatly resilient, likened, by one admirer, to Napoleon or Catherine of Russia. I decided to explore the life of Mrs Stevenson in more detail and in doing so, compiled a small collection of poems that emerged as a pamphlet in January 2016.

Fanny spent a great part of her married life looking after Stevenson, booking yachts, cooking meals, planting gardens, finding doctors, always vigilant in case his fragile health was endangered, sometimes to the chagrin of his literary friends. Strong-willed by nature, Fanny often adopted the position of overseer, and, in Samoa, she even became a sort of doctor to the locals, curing their ills with medicines she had gathered in her travels. Her husband called her a 'peasant' – a title that she did not like, but one that conveys the close connection she always formed with the natural landscape she inhabited.

The landscape surrounding the couple in their plantation in Apia, Samoa, was exotic and impenetrable. They sought to carve out a home from the thick creepers and abundant vegetation, which whirred with insects and held various sources of food, then not fully recorded. Fanny writes in her Samoan diary of 1891 about cooking some ferns she found in the bush for dinner. She describes Louis's reaction:

Louis began eating them, then stopped and asked me what certainty I had that the things were edible and not poisonous. I had either been told or had read that they made an excellent vegetable. But Louis persisted: how did I know what variety to gather? I didn't know, so gathered every kind that grew. Louis ate no more, but to find out whether they were poisonous or not I ate the whole dishful with an effort. I waked up in the night with a pain in my stomach and a most deathly feeling altogether.

(*Our Samoan Adventure*, p.94)

For me, this is a prime example of Fanny's strength of character. Louis doesn't want them; but they could be a potential source of food, so Fanny insists on eating them anyway. Later she remembers a chemist she encountered who spoke of men who had died from eating an 'overdose' of fern seed, so that night she lay believing her life to be hanging in the balance – something that Stevenson himself also frequently experienced. However, her old pioneering instincts had not let her down, and she got up the next day, 'none the worse' for the 'foolish experiment'.

My poem describes this incident, but I hoped to capture more than the facts evident in the diary. I pictured the domestic scene: the couple sitting over the plate of ferns and her decision to eat them. I wanted to portray her resolute nature in her simple actions: cleaning her plate; putting back the pan; pouring a glass of water; and then walking slowly to bed, all the time carrying the burden of anxiety that she might have just poisoned herself. As the poem progresses, Fanny becomes more isolated, having to face the consequences of her decision alone in the darkness, exposed suddenly to the 'exotic' and foreign landscape around her: the insects and wildlife (reported in a different diary extract) encroach upon her in her solitude: 'red ants', 'tree frogs', giant moths all work to amplify the unknown and frightening territory she has become exposed to in eating the ferns, but also in moving to Samoa, a far-off island, in order to preserve the health of her ailing husband – both actions involved a great deal of risk. The crying sound that I imagined her hearing in her stupor perhaps connects to the crying of a child she had so often heard during other difficult nights, nursing Stevenson, and further back to her youngest child Hervey who died in her care in Paris. It also might evoke the child she could never have with Stevenson – the fact that they had separate bedrooms is also conveyed in the poem.

The final image of the 'fire', something hazardous, turning into 'sunrise' – a symbol of hope and new beginnings – is one that is fitting for a life of adventure, of daring exploits, which, for her, didn't end in disaster but in fresh starts, new relationships, new continents and new gardens. I felt it was important to convey the sense of Fanny's isolation in this poem in an effort to depict a spirit that was always an independent one. As a woman of that period she had to endure so much alone, and 1894 she was left to begin again after Louis's death, going on to outlive him by twenty years.

This project allowed me to step into someone else's shoes, which was a liberating experience. I kept the third person narrative as I felt there had to be an element of distance: as soon as I write 'I' in a poem, it always carries a sense of self and I wanted her persona to be the main presence. The poems capture vignettes from Mrs Stevenson's life and lay them before the reader like pictures from a heroic journey undertaken by many other 'wives' so often in the shadow of their accomplished husbands.

Ferns' is taken from *An Ember from the Fire: Poems on the Life of Fanny Van de Grift Stevenson* (Poetry Salzburg, January 2016)

Ferns

She cooked them with lime juice and butter.
Tiny spirals melted,
slopped from the spoon like spinach.
She breathed in their bitterness.
At six she served them
with hard bread and onions.
She knew from his face
and the way he pushed each one
to the side of the plate
that he was thinking of poison –
those boys who died in the bush.

He watched her stab them
with her fork, lips glistening
she swallowed the lot.
After dinner he heard her
lift the copper pan to its hook,
pour some water from the jug,
her steady steps on the stair.

That night her stomach burned,
red ants danced through her blood.
She sweated into her clothes,
listening to the tree frog cry like a child,
and later a moth the size of a hummingbird
rested on her bed.
She thought she saw fire in its eye,
but in the drowsy coolness
it became a splinter of sunrise
caught in a giant unblinking lens.

DAVID
CONSTANTINE

DAVID CONSTANTINE

My Tilley Hat

Tom Stockin, forgive me, I am wearing your Tilley hat.
It blew out of the sea on a storm-force westerly
At Popplestone into a field already sown
With cuttlefish, plastic, pizzles of oarweed, a dead seal
And stones that would break every bone in your body. Your hat
When I ran after it, rose, flew, flopped, rose up again
Like a spent bird. But in the end I nabbed it. Sodden
It was, sodden and smeared, and host to a multitude
Of small worms that had entered through a rip in the crown.
Tom Stockin, till then I never knew I wanted a Tilley hat
But now: How did I manage without? I washed it thoroughly
In soapy water, evicted the beasties, and closed
The head wound with a silver tape. A hat's a hat
They say, and that is that. Unless it's a Tilley hat.
Your name's in the lining, clear, indelibly
With a telephone number half decipherable.
Should I try harder to contact you? I tell myself
You are very likely drowned and what if I got your widow
Or some other loved one? Too distressing. But to be honest
Now that I know I've always wanted a Tilley hat
And the furious January gales have delivered me one
I'm not sure I want you or your descendants
Informed of where it made landfall. I never take it off
Except in the evenings if there's nothing on television
I might study the account of its manufacture and virtues

Printed in English and French over the inner crown
And – bless you for this, Tom – an old love of languages
Revives in me: I see myself at teatime in short trousers
Reading from the HP Sauce bottle to my astonished parents:
This high quality sauce... *Cette sauce de haute qualité* ...
And now these evenings alone by the driftwood fire
Imagine me, Tom, reading aloud to the lares and penates:
It floats, ties on, repels rain, won't shrink ... *Il flotte*
S'attache, protège contre la pluie, ne rétrécit pas ...
I know it by heart, Tom, in the two tongues: *le chapeau Tilley*
Made in Canada, *fait au Canada*. I have even wondered
Did you say goodbye to it on your Eastern seabord, or mid-Atlantic?
Strange things happen. There's a buoy I can see at low water
Through this very window, beached here a century ago
From the Saint Lawrence river. Are you out there, Tom,
Sunk and your Tilley hat floated? Tom Stockin
It is my intention to be cremated in this Tilley hat
And to have my ashes scattered when the wind is easterly
So that if you are indeed lying full fathom five
In a sense you and I may meet and your Tilley hat
After a fashion will be returned to you, Tom Stockin.

High wind, sunset, high spring tide

Water-fire, tongued up and whirling
And bodies of water in the appearance of hard turquoise
Slipping into milk, into flocks of snow, a small rain
Ghosts in the look of rainbows and tasting of salt

And the din of it, the sun must roar like that
Out of which it has travelled across an ocean
With the wind behind it, the long fetch
Of the shapes of chaos, the makings, unmakings

None aspiring to another condition, all
Bound for ever in the play of the laws of flux
Which are fine and various, beyond calculation
And immutable. With that savage landfall

For a while I stood level and wrack
Ripped from its tenure was held up heraldic
Tined, branching and fingering on a white crest
For my brief contemplation and in a broken dazzle

Along with stones as rounded as cannonballs came
Flung in also, bloody, a seal pup
And when the blanket of the foam withdrew
There he lay, nosing towards our so-called terra firma

This creature very adept in its given element
Delivered gashed and pumping with hot blood
Into a bay as small as my span of years
That embraces as I do a speck of the possible

Chaos drove, the dance that haunts our blood
And the holes of the eyes and the curious brain took it in
A little, its breath ripped mine from my mouth
And I clutched at straws of our difference

Love, grief

The lucky and the unlucky

1
That was the evening the *Grace* appeared
At the mouth of the sound, a brave phenomenon
Blue and orange on the white water
Between the two sheer headlands, nosed around
And leaving then she left our vision opening
Into an Atlantic vacant of humanity.

Northwest, half a hemisphere was quilting over
Flocks, hanks, shreds of woolly softness burning
Chillier than the sea. Those moonless nights
We woke and heard in the hectic breathless zones
The cold and furious serpents of the winds
That circle us all, the lucky and the unlucky.

2
That was the afternoon and that the low water.
Wreck there was none. Tomorrow maybe?
Making from shore to point across the weed
My looking intersected with the time of day
The light, the slant on a small pale floor of sand
Where a lifted skirt of wrack had swirled aside.

High-vis, the coastguards rounded the point with staves
And phones looking along the tideline. We enjoyed
A conversation I've enjoyed before:
The wind, the currents, the tide ebbing or flowing…
Some never come up. But warming in my fist:
Faustina; Light-bearing Diana, scried through verdigris.

3
This is the morning, there our little boat
Red and white she rides a jade inrushing sea
Rocks and lifts and seems to fight the mooring
Her partner and exciter in the dance
Among the billion tongues of water-fire
Full in the sun-struck, sun-outflashing race

Of this new day's unstoppable pentecost. Oh swimmer
Lover that you were of solitary moonlight dips
While the *Emerald Dawn* goes through to the fishing grounds
And you are lost and turning still somewhere below her wake
I see the washed-out ghost of you at heaven's window
Pining for Earth, the blue, the lovely-watery.

Note: Eyes down, looking for nothing, at very low water I found a
Roman coin: Faustina, wife of Marcus Aurelius, on one side, Diana
Lucifera on the other. Then I met the coastguards, looking for a young
man, a swimmer, who had gone missing. He washed in long after they
had given up looking.

ESSAY

ON THE OUTSIDE

Conor McCormack

Conor McCormack is a Bristol-based filmmaker, writer and psycho-analyst. For three years he has documented the Bristol Hearing Voices Network – a self-help group for people who hear voices and have other unusual experiences.

*The result of this collaboration is **In the Real**, a documentary film which goes right to the heart of the voice-hearing experience, exploring the ways voice-hearers negotiate the complex deadlocks of psychosis and help each other to make sense of their unusual experiences.*

***In the Real** was supported creatively and financially by Hearing the Voice, an interdisciplinary study of voice hearing based at Durham University, funded by the Wellcome Trust.*

've always been drawn to making films about people who are on the outside of things. It's from outside, from the perspective of the person who is excluded, that you get the best view on society as a whole. A lot of people who hear voices and people with a diagnosis of schizophrenia and/or psychosis have that outsider's perspective of watching the world from elsewhere somehow.

A lot of what I read is to do with questions of how one knows oneself, who one is for the other, the subject-object relationship: these aren't abstract intellectual issues for the people in this film, these are actually pressing, *lived* experiences and concerns for them.

ERROL BEHIND BARS

The DSM – *Diagnostic and Statistical Manual of Mental Disorders* – gets bigger and bigger each time it's published, with new names for conditions that are essentially just lists of symptoms and there is so much cross-over between all of these things that eventually they become meaningless titles. It's a failed attempt at creating generalised categories for what are very *particular* human experiences: I wanted to explore those experiences in this film and give a voice to those people who live them.

By denying a person's reality it's almost like you're taking away part of their soul.
Errol – participant in the film

Psychosis takes you to the limit of what can be understood through the medical discourse – it takes you to the point where that kind of understanding breaks down, because medical science is good at talking about facts and things that are measurable and have some kind of concrete existence, but it's not so good at talking about how people generate meaning in their lives. There is always a big discordance between how somebody who experiences psychosis talks about it and how mental health professionals or doctors talk about it. What a doctor might describe as being delusion, is also a deeply held belief, someone's own construction that they use to make sense of the world and position themselves in it; it's a real part of their being.

In psychiatric terms, the primary symptoms are categorised as being the onset of an illness (if you want to think about it as an illness), so in this case, the first time someone hears voices, which can initially be an extremely perplexing, senseless experience. The secondary symptoms are the person's own *response* to that, their own effort at making meaning and sense out of it. There is a problem in that anti-psychotic medication makes no distinction between primary and secondary symptoms: it just zonks people out. It leaves no room for the story that the person has created to explain their situation; those stories are often something creative, something useful and something that should be encouraged, I think.

A belief always has a purpose behind it, it does something, it holds something in place. Secondary symptoms can piece things together and are a kind of creative response to an emptiness and a void and something that's unthinkable.

After a week or so (in hospital) I think to myself 'Why am I here, if I'm someone special?' And after that it's just like I dismiss everything, I dismiss all my past beliefs, all my spirituality, and I'm in a place where everything I believed is a lie. So who am I? Where do I fit in? How do I feel about things? I'm kind of left with this part that's just hurting, really hurting. It's pain that's mental, that's physical, that's spiritual; it's fear. Before I was on top of the world and then when you realise it's not true, it's like... I'm just a mad person, a schizophrenic.

Rene – participant in the film

People always ask me, 'What impact would you like this film to have?' and I think the film just speaks for itself, I'm not sure what I would like it to do. But certainly, within clinical settings there are certain kinds of imperatives and ways of doing things whereby sometimes people don't get listened to, or get overlooked and the diagnosis comes to dominate everything – that needs looking at. The first duty of a clinician is just not to make things worse and a lot of the time that's what happens – people go into the mental health system seeking some kind of answer (patients and practitioners) and they have no idea what they're letting themselves in for. One thing I would like the film to model, is to get people to try and listen, you know? To listen and respect people's beliefs and differences and try not to look at things in the kind of reductive binaries of good and bad, inside and outside, positive and negative. I've gone into hospitals and screened the film to hardened, old-school psychiatrists, and some have said to me "This has changed the way I think about my practice" and I think that's because the film shows something of the lived, human experience behind and beyond the diagnosis. It shows you people rather than patients.

In the Real will be shown at the World Hearing Voices Congress in Paris, Oct 19th–22nd and is available for screenings elsewhere. See www.inthereal.org

POETRY

THE OLD POEM

Brian Nellist

William Shakespeare (1564–1616),
Hamlet Prince of Denmark, I. i. 1–13

Enter Bernardo and Francisco, two sentinels
BERNARDO Who's there?
FRANCISCO
    Nay, answer me. Stand, and unfold yourself.
BERNARDO Long live the king!
FRANCISCO Bernardo?
BERNARDO He.
FRANCISCO
    You come most carefully upon your hour.
BERNARDO
    'Tis now struck twelve. Get thee to bed, Francisco.
FRANCISCO
    For this relief much thanks. 'Tis bitter cold,
    And I am sick at heart.
BERNARDO
    Have you had quiet guard?
FRANCISCO
                    Not a mouse stirring.
BERNARDO
    Well, good night.
    If you do meet Horatio and Marcellus,
    The rivals of my watch, bid them make haste.

ON SHAKESPEARE'S *HAMLET*

Surely, you might say, if you're going to choose lines from *Hamlet* in celebration of four hundred years of Shakespeare you should take them from a soliloquy or the death of Ophelia. But he is a dramatic poet where it's not simply a matter of verbal beauty or density but how the words create not just a specific situation but an almost visual sensation of what it involves. The play would be first performed in summer daylight but with breath-taking boldness we are compelled to imagine midnight uncertainty and bitter cold. The jerky exchange between the sentries at once intimates a present threat yet this is also a group of friends meeting. Francisco is on duty so it should be he who challenges the newcomer yet when he tells Bernardo 'Unfold yourself' it is either that he is muffled up against the cold or is like a conspirator or has his identity under question. 'Long live the king' comes the reply as though he might not. Somewhere buried in the lines is the regularity of iambic pentameter but the spasmodic irregularity, the jerkiness of the exchanges constitutes the meaning of the passage more than the actual words. ''Tis bitter cold / And I am sick at heart'. Not 'So I am' but 'And' as though it were a separate unexplained fact. No wonder Bernardo asks if anything untoward has happened; 'Not a mouse stirring'. The response seems in excess of the circumstance. T. S. Eliot famously criticised the play for its lack of an adequate objective correlative. But surely that is the point. Reactions throughout are in excess of their causes; almost as though the feelings have to create the reason for their existence. Francisco's 'sick at heart' is a gratuitously personal comment in an official exchange. It establishes that mood of uncertainty, that interrogation of identity that marks the play, all in the first thirteen lines. These are not simply dramatic poems as L. C. Knight claimed long ago but throat-grabbing dramas, even in the theatre of a reader's mind.

KIM DEVEREUX

© Bid Jones

BEAUTY IN EVERY WRINKLE

Kim Devereux

R ecently plus-size model Ashley Graham made it on to the cover page of a sports magazine. Wahey! This will finally help us over-size-10ers feel that our abnormal bodies are vaguely normal. Except, my flab looks just the same to me: flab-non-grata! And no talent scout has come knocking on its wobbly gates.

I must admit, there was a brief moment of joy when I first saw Ashley in a swim suit. 'She's even fatter than me,' I thought happily. But when I noticed her toned legs and her confident look I reached for the nearest rice cake, with butter and honey to make it count.

Ashley Graham
on the cover of *Sports Illustrated*

I get hot under the collar when I hear that body image issues will be cured by replacing emaciated models with so-called 'ordinary' women or models with a healthier height to weight ratio. Am I a covert fat body fascist? Do I enjoy cream-cake flavoured trips into guilt? Do I resent, in some Freudian twist, letting go of the idea that my life will sort itself out once I have attained physical perfection? No, this particular hope languishes along with my unused scales in a dusty cupboard.

I simply believe that nothing short of changing the very way we look at bodies can stop this madness. What we need is Rembrandt's eyes. Something happened to me over the period of two years while I was working on my novel *Rembrandt's Mirror.* I have a particular approach to writing. It's like method acting. There are actors who can slip into character as soon as the director says 'action'. Others have to torture themselves to get and stay in character – even while queuing for the toilet. I belong to the latter lot. I did my homework to get into Rembrandt's head and then wandered around Tesco mystified there were no decent chunks of cheese or herring to be had.

Anyway, jokes aside, I started to see through his eyes and gazed at the woman he loved. She was beautiful and not just her, every woman, every man and every child he/I drew or painted moved me in some way (with the exception of Geertje Dircx – but that's another story). Then strangely my friends started becoming more beautiful and even my own mirror proffered a passable reflection. 'Weird s***,' I concluded.

Furthermore my brain became bemused by words such as fat, thin, plus-sized, hourglass, pear-shaped, small hips, large hips, full-bosomed or flat. These bizarre categories reminded me of Hugh Fearnley-Wittingstall making a rather good point in front of a twenty-ton pile of freshly dug up parsnips in a Norfolk farmyard, 'They have been consigned to the rubbish heap purely because they don't look pretty enough.' He lamented. 'It's one of the most shocking things I've ever seen. And they aren't even wonky, or bruised or deformed in any way.'

I felt upset for him and those rejected parsnips. So what's behind this choosiness of ours? What we see and how we see is predicated by what we think we want or need; be it food to survive on a desert island or a new car that tickles our fancy. Perception is both selective and creative. It is influenced by a great many factors;

our mood, peer pressure, context and the learned habits we adopt over time.

There are upsides and downsides; the ability to tailor our perception is very helpful when on a long walk and looking for something to chow down on but results in a self-defeating mess if we look at our own body as a utility.

Our body then becomes merely a means to attract the right partner or to become accepted as a member of a group – in short; to be 'in'. If I view my body in this way then my happiness becomes dependent on fitting into the latest fashion. Role-models become very important. But buying into them is like accepting a self-perpetuating virus that spawns system-wide misery.

If we embrace the idea of looking like Beyoncé or Ashley Graham, we begin to judge ourselves according to what is really a random set of criteria (weight, size etc). Of course this point has been made before, but it tends to be made only about overly thin role-models. I grant some role models are more helpful than others but even with a more healthy role-model our perception narrows to the point where we no longer see the million and one assets that make our personal parsnip beautiful.

By virtue of the fact that there is only one Beyoncé or Ashley Graham on the planet and by wanting to become like her we are set up for disappointment. We've become a supermarket buyer with an insane set of criteria and end up rejecting our own body that has absolutely nothing wrong with it. We've trained ourselves *out* of seeing our own beauty, the way Pavlov's poor dog was trained *into* salivating at the sound of a bell.

There is only one of you on the planet and the only role model that exists for being you – is *you*.

So in order to truly escape our perceptual prison we need to learn to see in an entirely new way. Despite these liberating thoughts, I soon hit a road block in the shape of Rembrandt's *Seated female nude*, from around 1631.

Boy was she ugly. Just look at that mass of stomach cascading down her torso like molten cheese. Twenty-five year old Rembrandt really ought to have lavished his talents on a more worthy subject. Even Rembrandt's contemporaries – who were well used to Rubens' fleshy nudes – thought this lady was a bit of an imposition on the eye. It must have taken some effort to find this blob. And this wasn't a quick dash of a drawing. This

RP-P-1961-1109

Rembrandt, *Seated Nude*, 1629–1633 © Rijksmuseum, Amsterdam

etching would have taken days of toil and effort. As evidenced by the displeasure of his contemporaries Rembrandt was not catering to the market; no, he was pleasing himself (as per usual). He was chomping at the bit to preserve the indentations on her calve left by her stockings for posterity. As far as I was concerned, the master had some explaining to do. I conjured up a scene where Hendrickje, his housemaid, overhears Rembrandt teaching his students. Hendrickje is the central character in my novel, *Rembrandt's Mirror*. She is a young woman from a strict Calvinist family and after entering Rembrandt's household she is slowly drawn to him by his freshness, his freedom and by his fierce intensity.

'He pointed at the model. 'Can you see the indentations on her lower thighs from wearing garters? Don't miss them out, or any other detail; don't call it ugly or beautiful. Study her with the same care as you would search for a painful but tiny splinter of glass in your finger.

Let each line of her body draw your attention, just as the nagging pain of the splinter compels you to look for it with the utmost attentiveness.

You are a lot of lazy gawkers. Rouse yourselves, for if you miss one mark, one line, one shadow, one curve – you will miss out on knowing this particular woman, right here in front of you, and what have you got then? Nothing. And worse, whoever looks at your drawing will also miss out on knowing her, but not only her – he will miss out on knowing life itself and he will feel cheated. Worst of all, he won't part with a stuiver for your work.'

[...]

Then Rembrandt added, 'Once you know every single line on her body by heart and can draw her blind, then the invisible part of her will be revealed to you. Her true beauty. Then you will be able to draw her perfectly, using only a handful of strokes with your pencil. But until then you need to lovingly draw each and every wrinkle.'

I left the room quietly as they settled back down to work. What had he meant by her true beauty? If even the ugliest of

the streetwalkers possessed it, did Geertje possess it? Did I possess it? The invisible, a lovely word, so full of promise.
I went down to the kitchen and started peeling apples. The redness of the peel, the wormholes, the frayed edges where my knife had cut – all of it exquisite. Instead of placing all the pieces in the pot to be conserved for the winter, I started devouring them immediately.

(From *Rembrandt's Mirror* by Kim Devereux)

Like Hendrickje, I longed to see this true beauty. However – full disclosure – I was still regularly fantasising about time-travelling to the mid-eighties to conduct a close up contemplation of Tom Selleck's shapely legs. More fittingly described as poetry, perfection and sexiness incarnate.

As for the Rembrandt bit of me… I started to struggle with the essentials of UK living; I became inept at talking about the weather. When an old lady commented on the rather pretty fog rolling in from the sea I caused a conversational dry spell because I was riveted by the pretty little scar on the side of her nose. Never mind; it's the seeing that matters!

'Real Beauty'

The Dove 'Real Beauty Campaign' has its ten-year anniversary this year. The ads depict ordinary women making a case for their 'real beauty'. Except those 'ordinary' women were hand-picked by talent scouts. If you place them next to Rembrandt's seated nude, they look about as ordinary as a Waitrose carrot. They look like a roll call of a present-day beauty wish list: youthful, smiley, sans cellulite – and the one on the left is definitely holding in her stomach. Wait a minute, they all are!

They are of course posed to make the most of their assets and the least of their bulgy bits. Rembrandt's nude, by contrast, is plonked on a stool, unclassical and utterly revealing of her 'imperfections'. The Dove ad, like its products, reeks of sanitizing efforts; Rembrandt's nude exudes the heartening aroma of authenticity. She's just walked into the studio, taken off her clothes and sat down with a sigh. She's a convincing combination of unease and not-bothered. She's not pandering because nobody is asking her to. Rembrandt finds his jewel in the same way that Zen practitioners

Dove Campaign for Real Beauty

do. The most vivid and beautiful experience lies in simply seeing what's in front of one's nose.

'Seeing things as it is.'
(Shunryū Suzuki)

By contrast, in the Dove ad the photographer, like a puppeteer, is pulling the strings from behind the lens. Rembrandt's women don't smile except to please themselves. They possess the power that comes from not trying to be something they are not.

On to my most hated ad ever.

Are you beach body ready?

Last year's 'Are you Beach Body Ready?' campaign by Protein World attracted 378 complaints to the ASA on the grounds that the poster implied other body shapes were inferior. The complaints were not upheld and the campaign is being run again this year.

Let's juxtapose the ad and Rembrandt's painting of *Woman Bathing in a Stream*. This exercise could be seen as a little unfair; after all Rembrandt was trying to sell paintings not protein powder. It doesn't really matter because both have chosen to depict women and whenever someone depicts a woman it tells you something about them.

Rembrandt, *A Woman bathing in a Stream*,
1654 © The National Gallery, London

Protein World
'Are you Beach Body Ready' ad campaign

The woman depicted by Rembrandt is assumed to be Hendrickje Stoffels, whom I mentioned earlier.

The model in the Protein World ad is Renee Somerfield. Despite her full-frontal stance and confrontational gaze she appears to have been pinned to a board by an eager collector. Hendrickje is mid movement, wading into a stream. Despite taking weeks to paint, Rembrandt's work has fluidity and a snap-shot feeling about it.

There is no sense of Renee as a person. It took several Google searches to unearth her name. By contrast volumes have been written about the identity of the woman bathing. It is thought that the painting sticks two fingers up at the church council which was giving Hendrickje a hard time for living with Rembrandt out of wedlock. The story goes, Rembrandt painted Hendrickje as the nymph Callisto, who was seduced by Zeus, cast out from Diana's retinue but later redeemed by Zeus and afforded an eternal place of honour in the night sky.

Renee is there for her 'unbelievable body', as she describes it herself on her website. Hendrickje is there for both her physical and psychological presence. Art historian Eric van Slueter points out that Rembrandt's main purpose was not to emulate classical rules but to incite the greatest possible empathy in the viewer.

Empathy is our ability to share the feelings of others, even fictional others. We take our cue from Hendrickje's relaxed body, her smile and her surroundings. Rembrandt further enlists our imagination through the way the water ripples against her calves, causing us to remember the physical sensations we once felt wading into water. Before we know it Rembrandt has us palpably sensing and feeling Hendrickje's experience. At the same time we continue to look on her from the outside. In doing both at the same time, the separateness of seeing and being seen is transcended. The outer is subsumed in the inner and vice versa, like whisked egg-white folded into dough. Rembrandt's cake is ready to rise.

This effect is underpinned by other tricks of the trade which enlist our collaboration – our Beholder's Share as Gombrich called it – in bringing the painting to life. Rembrandt uses broad and rough brushstrokes of shades of cream and ochre and leaves it to our eyes and mind to assemble them into the folds of her shift. Her face, much like the Mona Lisa's smile is half-hidden in shade. It is this vagueness which compels us to imagine and emote her facial expression. This is a far more involving way of going about things than if he had painted everything in great detail.

Rembrandt's assistant, Samuel van Hoogstraten advises, 'Do not concern yourselves too much with small details of shadows. [...] In the same way that a man, catching sight of his friend from a distance or meeting him in twilight, straight away sees his appearance in his mind and recognises him, so a rough sketch can often create such a great impression on beholders that they can see more in it than is actually there.'

A composite reality is created, augmented by our own feelings, beliefs and visual completion of her appearance. And in playing our part, we become invested, perhaps even see something of ourselves reflected in his art.

So why is *Woman bathing in a Stream* an unusual and unconventional depiction of a woman? You only have to survey western art, or even present-day advertising, to find that the majority of portraits of women can easily be categorised into: nurse, mother, best friend, sister, virgin, whore or ball-buster and so on. It is rare to find examples of a woman who is depicted simultaneously as a psychologically present human being and sexually attractive. Women tend to be depicted either in one of the roles listed above or as sexual objects. Rembrandt defies our pigeon-holing habits.

He unifies – wholly and holily – Hendrickje's sensuality, sexual attractiveness and her humanity.

On the one hand what Rembrandt is doing is not a big deal. It's just seeing what is; Women are integrated human beings. They are not exclusively this or that. On the other hand he is breaking the mould because to this day most religious and patriarchal societies still treat the combination of a woman's personhood and her sexuality as if it were semtex, i.e. it's best to keep the ingredients separate and under wraps.

The great escape

So how to escape these mind-forged manacles? My proposal is that we teach men and women to see with Rembrandt's eyes. We ought to make live drawing classes part of the national curriculum. It is one of the best ways of learning to see what bodies really look like. When drawing from life you realise, willy-nilly, that our bodies are animated by our hearts and souls and that's when you start seeing beauty in every wrinkle.

I've mentioned above the capacity of Rembrandt's art to evoke an experience for the viewer where the distinction between the observer and the observed melts away: we are looking at Hendrickje, we are being Hendrickje and we are seeing ourselves too in Rembrandt's mirror and we are being seen by ourselves. It's like some crazy koan that causes our rational, predictive, linear mind to roll over in disgust and defeat. What remains is a gap, a crack in the known, and through it we sniff the air of freedom.

Last year in the National Gallery, when I stood in front of the little painting once again, it dawned on me that for all of Hendrickje's absorption, she is also aware of Rembrandt's eyes on her. She is in relationship with his gaze as she is in relationship with the wind that wafts over her body.

This is a woman who has grown up with a hefty dose of Calvinist guilt and yet the male gaze that holds her does not diminish her. Rembrandt's way of seeing is not passive or laid-back. It is active, warm and fresh, like the sunlight dappled forest that surrounds her.

I think I've just taken a great many pages to say that, quite simply, we need to see – and be seen – with eyes of love.

'Does for Rembrandt what *Girl with a Pearl Earring* did for Vermeer.' *Mail on Sunday*

Rembrandt's Mirror

KIM DEVEREUX

ECHOES

I'd been walking around for days perplexed in my spare moments by two quotations that stayed out of reach but which felt strongly connected. It was only when I started in the most garbled and fumbling way (since I couldn't lay hold of either) to ask someone 'Where do these odd words come from?' that both turned up intact in my mind. They are two of the most well-known and important quotations in the English language. I don't know how I forgot them.

In 1948 Nye Bevan said:

The NHS will last as long as there are folk left with the faith to fight for it.

Several centuries before, Shakespeare concluded sonnet No.18 ('Shall I compare thee to a summer's day?') with these lines:

So long as men can breathe, or eyes can see,
So long lives this, and this gives life to thee.

There's almost nothing more to say. I love the thought that Bevan must have had that same echo in his ears when he projected forward his hope for the NHS. Reaching *back* in time, reaching *deep* into his sense of the human spirit, reaching for Shakespeare who was also reaching *forward* to the unborn, urgent, living act, Bevan imagined his creation would be safe. He was sure of it.

ONE-PAGER

POETRY

STUART PICKFORD

Washing Up

The anaesthetist smiles:
You'll only feel like
someone's washing up
inside your stomach.

She shoots morphine
into *your lovely spine*,
strokes your cheeks
and calls your name
from the rim of darkness.

This time, no stirrups,
bed pans, bastard swearing,
you thrashing like a fish
held down in air.

At 7.13, the magician
reaches in to lift out
life. Our baby's gripped
by his heels and bleats
as he's weighed.

Womb-curved, slimy,
floating in my arms,
a boy, a son, our son.
You little bugger, you say.

On his breathing skin,
creams, blood
and my purged fears
shed as tears.

Nursery

The study has to go, my
study with 70s roses,
blistered gloss and damp
leaching the chimney breast.
My garden shed, smelling
of dusty books and me.

A bubble of pine sap
from Thunder Bay, my fossil
of a cockle shell, small
as a pea, bagged, boxed.

Empty, sounds bounce.
These last days:
the pendulum of the brush.

The finishing touch:
a clip-framed watercolour
of a mob of kangaroos
painted by your mum.

The cot's instructions
baffle an afternoon until
it's perfect. Your room's
done. The first thing
I've done for you.

Now to rest, imagine
your vanilla scent,
mustard stools, brittle
cry, your wobbling face.
Alive and so light,
you filling this space.

THE READING REVOLUTION

THE LESSON

Alexis McNay

'We're absolute beginners, with nothing much at stake'

My son gets two costumes for Christmas and spends the day as Buzz Lightyear, Raphael from the Ninja Turtles (not his favourite of the four brothers, but Mikey has nunchucks, and Hugo prefers the twin daggers) and, mainly, himself. He's two. He has a button on his Buzz suit, which when he presses it produces the Space Ranger's motto, reproduced by Hugo as 'Finty a-Beyon!', at which point I hoist him into the air and orbit the house with him at shoulder height. This is hard work quite quickly at my age, but I get a boost from his absolute belief that he is flying and from that mantra of possibility which he chants in my ear.

Though my arms are tired, I'm reluctant to put him down; his joy is some bolster, but there's also no doubt a thought for when I might not be able – or around – to hold him up. One day he'll have to negotiate for himself a landscape far murkier than a Pixar film, and the moral certitude with which he now flies and I now guide will be challenged, over and over. There are, of course, signs that he's already sussing or sassing some of the vagaries of morality.

A couple of times I've picked him up from nursery and been told that he's been a little too handy with his hands. 'Kind hands', his keyworker asks me to remind him. But he also has little scratches on his face sometimes and I wonder whether he has been chastised for losing a little of the benevolence of his hands in self-defence. Or maybe it's too much Ninja Turtles. Either way, I'm confident at least that Hugo grows in a family that will provide him with love and the kind of well-meaning guidance that will – what? One would like to say that it's better than an upbringing in a dysfunctional family, but the world is a dysfunctional environment if you really look at it, and the most powerful lesson is not necessarily the one that teaches right.

When I was reading on the vulnerable prisoners wing at Walton prison a relatively new member of the group once said to me, 'How come you always bring in stories with a moral?' It was a rhetorical question and his implication was clear. 'Show me a story without a moral', I replied. As he came to know me better I know he realised I wasn't one for moralising in that conventional sense, nor did I select reading to instruct. If anything, prison taught me of the need to compromise and extemporise, no jurisdiction for morals formed in an easier world. I became almost friends with a man serving life for murder. It took me a long time to earn his trust. I was most disappointed in him, and in a great little regular group of which he was a kind of nucleus, when he and they were less than welcoming of a man attending the group for the first time. I knew from the group's reaction that this new man was a sexual offender, likely a paedophile. Of all the difficulties that this opened up, the most troubling was my own need to overcome the burden of expectation that I had placed on this group and its individuals. It was supposed to be inclusive, an enclave of tolerance, where the activity of reading together would unveil a common humanity. But I also knew the size – impossibility, it seemed sometimes – of the task on a wing comprised of about 20% sex offenders and the rest mostly young lads to thirties men on the VP for drug debt or violence which made them a target for reprisal. What held on the wing was a moral hierarchy not unlike that in larger society, with paedophiles bottom of the pecking order, though the stakes here were considerably higher. I took an opportunity when there were just the two of us around to sound out my almost friend discreetly on this problem; I was hoping with his influence, and with the respect I felt he had for me, that he might help if I could make him see my predicament. I remember what he told me very clearly: 'Don't get involved in that'. He was not warning me off, but he was offering advice, and in his way, on his turf, he was right. I remember the way he very succinctly put the case, from the crude statement of his own depth of feeling against that kind of offender, to the nuanced understanding that even someone with sympathy ought to be seen to be hostile toward them, since the wing is always watching, seeking out weakness. I understood. I told him so, but that I would have to insist on a semblance of civility, which he understood. And so we went on, strained sometimes, fractious others, with me refereeing, shushing down murmurings that might develop otherwise into open warfare or verbal lynching, trying to lead by example in offering everyone who entered the room the same level of respect and open aspect. Sometimes it worked, as if by miracle. But I remember once having to exclude three scouse lads, who might equally have benefitted from the reading, because they were gesturing behind the back of a man's head, their hands formed into pistols, their thumbs cocking, their mouths blowing off noiseless gunshots. I remember, too, how the man in for murder became an almost friend, how I read with him for several months, how he tidied the room after the session, how once he gestured for me to enter his cell to show me his 'home' and the pictures of his family, and how he was shipped out to another prison from one week to the next without a goodbye.

Toni Cade Bambara's *The Lesson* presents a few problems, not least the extent to which one tries to deploy an African American accent when reading it, not least with a group of white blokes in Walton prison. There's also the problem of locating the lesson, and that's what I like about it. There's Miss Moore, and her attempts to stir up the nascent class/race/dollar awareness of her young charges, but this is a lesson that Bambara has Sylvia subvert with her theft of the taxi change (though I like the ending, with Sylvia determining to make time and space 'to think this day through'). The price tag on a toy yacht is a kind of crime against humanity, but Sylvia knows how to survive and will use the playground politics of class, weight, sexuality and any leverage to hand to work the hierarchy and maintain ascendancy over her peers, as well as a bit of sleight-of-hand to fund a barbecue. She has absorbed from somewhere already the lesson that in an immoral, unequal world you take for yourself what is withheld. This wouldn't be satisfactory, if Sylvia were allowed to diss everything with the complete certitude reserved for the wrong, even if her age is some dispensation. But the story has this amazing bit, where Sylvia is stymied by the oppressive opulence of the toy shop, where we are made to feel the power of money and the inhibition of poverty, and then another amazing touch, where this feeling is paralleled to unworthiness in church. Then as now as ever, the poor, the unwashed. And there's your moral wanting a moral.

Miss Moore says they should go into the toy shop:

Only she don't lead the way. So me and Sugar turn the corner to where the entrance is, but when we get there I kinda hang back. Not that I'm scared, what's there to be afraid of, just a toy store. But I feel funny, shame, But what I got to be shamed about? Got as much right to go in as anybody. But somehow I can't seem to get hold of the door, so I step away from Sugar to lead. But she hangs back too, And I look at her and she looks at me and this is ridiculous. I mean, damn, I have never been shy about doing nothing or going nowhere. But then Mercedes steps up and then Rosie Giraffe and Big Butt crowd in behind and shove, and next thing we all stuffed into the doorway with only Mercedes squeezing past us, smoothing out her jumper and walking right down the aisle. Then the rest of us tumble in like a glued-together jigsaw done all wrong. And people look in at us. And it's like the time me and Sugar crashed into the Catholic church on a dare. But once we got in there and everything so hushed and holy and the candles and the bowin and the handkerchiefs on all the drooping heads, I just couldn't go through with the plan. Which was for me to run up to the altar and do a tap dance while Sugar played the nose flute and messed around in the holy water.

The sure step, the cockiness, the toughness that are Sylvia's inheritance aren't currency when she crosses these thresholds – the toy shop, the church – sudden demarcations that refract poise and identity into a jumbled puzzle. And it doesn't make sense, her irreverence made reverent like that, at least not to her. Something is being registered, though, insidiously, in these feelings of vulnerability and exclusion, but neither she nor we can quite know the value of the lesson, and we have the author to thank for that.

Here's Toni Cade Bambara on Wholesomeness Versus Hatred:

> The greatest challenge in writing, then, in the earlier stages was to strike a balance between candor, honesty, integrity, and truth – terms that are fairly synonymous for crossword puzzlers and thesaurus ramblers but hard to equate as living actions. Speaking one's mind, after all, does not necessarily mean one is in touch with the truth or even with the facts. Being honest and frank in terms of my own where – where I'm at a given point in my political/spiritual/etc. development – is not necessarily in my/our interest to utter, not necessarily in the interest of health, wholesomeness. Certain kinds of poisons, for example – rage, bitterness, revenge – don't need to be in the atmosphere, not to mention in my mouth. I don't, for example, hack up racists and stuff them in metaphorical boxes. I do not wish to lend them energy, for one thing. Though certainly there are 'heavies' that people my stories. But I don't, for example, conjure up characters for the express purpose of despising them, of breaking their humps in public. I used to be astounded at Henry James et al., so nice nasty about it, too, soooo refined. Gothic is of no interest to me. I try not to lend energy to building grotesqueries, depicting morbid relationships, dramatizing perversity. Folks come up to me 'lowing as how since I am a writer I would certainly want to hear blah, blah, blah, blah'. They dump shit all over me, tell me about every ugly overheard and lived-through nightmare imaginable. They've got the wrong writer. The kid can't use it. I straightaway refer them to the neighbourhood healer, certain that anyone so intoxicated would surely welcome a cleansing. But they persist – 'Hey, this is for real, square business. The truth.' I don't doubt that the horror tales are factual. I don't even doubt that ugly is a truth for somebody... somehow. But I'm not convinced that ugly is the truth that can save us, redeem us. The old folks teach that. Be triflin' and ugly and they say, 'Deep down, gal, you know that ain't right,' appealing

to a truth about our deep-down nature. Good enough for me. Besides, I can't get happy writing ugly weird. If I'm not laughing while I work, I conclude that I'm not communicating nourishment, since laughter is the most sure-fire healant I know. I don't know all my readers, but I know well for whom I write. And I want for them no less than I want for myself – wholesomeness.

Hugo will not have to deal with the hardships of the ghetto, be it Harlem or (I hope) prison, but he'll have his sensibilities and morals tested enough by living in the world. I hope he manages wholesomeness. I hope he can see and understand some of the constraints on the kind hands of others. I hope he can manage or overcome the challenge of his generation in seeing the magnitude of the moral task faced by humanity while having limited control to address it. I hope that when he realises the impossibility of always doing or even knowing the right thing he manages, like Buzz, to fall with style.

And here's a poem for counterpoint.

LETTY'S GLOBE

When Letty had scarce pass'd her third glad year,
   And her young artless words began to flow,
One day we gave the child a colour'd sphere
  Of the wide earth, that she might mark and know,
By tint and outline, all its sea and land.
  She patted all the world; old empires peep'd
Between her baby fingers; her soft hand
  Was welcome at all frontiers. How she leap'd,
  And laugh'd and prattled in her world-wide bliss;
But when we turn'd her sweet unlearned eye
On our own isle, she raised a joyous cry –
  'Oh! yes, I see it, Letty's home is there!'
  And while she hid all England with a kiss,
Bright over Europe fell her golden hair.

Charles Tennyson Turner

POETRY

VINCENT PARKER

Recessional

I start early, finish when they say.
The man from Time and Motion watches,
Scanning fear and taking notes.

I drink early because I can't be late.
But sleep brings no peace. My walls creak.
Will the chimney collapse into the flue
As my house swallows its own tongue?

These days friends and family find me
On their doorsteps at the strangest of hours.
I listen to their slipper'd shuffle in the hall
As I think of good reason to be there.

THE READING REVOLUTION

OUR MUTUAL LIFE

Grace Farrington

I n one of my first experiences of Shared Reading, I visited a group in which we read towards the end a poem by Brendan Kennelly, 'The Good'. It is a poem about a type of person, and how we might recognise who 'the good' are. Kennelly refers to 'the good' in the plural, as 'they', as if such individuals exist as a hidden category within the world. There is the feeling in the poem that these are numerous and yet uncounted. Kennelly simply affirms in the last two lines: 'I think that I know one or two / Among my friends.'

Fast forward six or seven years, and I find myself thinking about how easy it is to be caught confusingly between categories, in need of the kind of clarification that might be associated with 'the good'. Recent events have brought about one of the biggest political shake ups in my own lifetime, as Britain reels from the outcome of the referendum over our membership of the European Union. It is a time when the notion of community itself seems to be at stake, on perhaps at least two levels. The larger representations of community with which we have been familiar seem suddenly not to fit: there is discontent, confusion and division about the kind of Britain people want, and on how the country should represent itself to the international community, as it is termed. But there has also been a huge amount of exposure of underlying alignments – communities of opinion – that somehow cut across the relationships we hold with each other as members of our families, workplaces and neighbourhoods. More than the result of the vote itself, I have felt deeply disturbed by the level of opposition and judgement that has been stirred up by this process, by virtue of forcing people to take up a position on either side of a dividing line. There is the feeling that either you are on the right or the wrong side, and that you can be identified as such by stating your opinion. The private has become public, and unsightly for being so.

Attendees of Shared Reading groups sometimes joke that politics and religion are two topics from which we try to steer clear in our discussions, for fear of awakening these same divisions. But I am aware too that we each live in an atmosphere from which we sometimes cannot cut ourselves free, and so I am interested in what happened particularly in our reading groups on the morning following the vote on 23rd June. People came into my group strangely silent, and no one mentioned what had happened the night before until I asked one woman how she was, feeling that it was important somehow to get out of this stalemate. She began to open up the subject, speaking of how disheartened, disappointed and fearful she felt. Others were then able to join in, although I don't think we really returned to the subject once we had started reading.

I think sometimes people are worried about disturbing the peace, but it worries me more that we can settle for a quiet in which there is no real peace to rely upon. There is a need for places and spaces in which a particular kind of honesty can occur. In the opening scene of *King Lear*, in answer to her father's challenge to his daughters – 'Which of you shall we say doth love us most' – Cordelia claims the honesty of remaining silent against the pressure to pay her way using words and persuasive speech. Yet as an audience we do hear what Cordelia is trying to say, in a way that seems impossible for any character in the play other than Kent to achieve. In her asides, we are the first to hear of her own struggle to respond to the challenge, and she is in fact the only character at this stage to whom we are able to relate in this way. I am interested in the position in which this places us as an audience, and in how this ability to listen to people – almost by seeing them thinking – might potentially alter the perspective that we have of them. We may not agree with the response that Cordelia makes to her father here, and I know some feel it betrays a stubbornness in her that must be allowed to soften, but at the same time it does allow for a deeper understanding of how she feels in being called upon to respond to such a challenge.

I wonder if we can move from this idea of the position of the audience to that of a group leader; required sometimes to be an arbiter at moments of tension, difficulty or frustration within a Shared Reading group. One cannot always say what one thinks in these situations, and yet the thinking that is involved is important. A group leader shared with me for example his experience of running a group for parents with their young children at 9am on 24th June.

A dad who attends the group apologised in advance for if he yawned during the session as he'd been up all night watching the results. I tried to gauge whether he was sad or happy with the result. Before the group started properly a mum said that she felt sad at the result, at which point the dad said that he was very pleased and had been out campaigning for Leave. It was quite a tricky situation to be in – one mum speaking about her fears for the future while a dad tried convincing her that all would be well.

To be a gauge of the feeling is an essential part of the role of the Shared Reading group leader. I admire too how in this instance the person is looking out for signs of this before advancing or even bringing to mind his own feeling about the matter. Further, what is interesting about the dad is that his courteous apology comes first, and despite having been in campaigning mode, he arrives in the group in a different spirit, giving little indication of his own strong feeling about the result. It seems to be part of the learning curve of the Shared Reading group leader that one comes to accept that there is so much that we do not know about what our group members are carrying in their daily lives. On the other hand, the mum in this example is quite quick to give her response. Often this is how discussions in Shared Reading groups begin; a feeling is expressed and different members talk about whether they felt the same thing and where this seems to have come from. But in this instance the group leader expands on what made this tricky: 'There was definitely a hint of tension, I think because the dad was so sure it was a good thing while the mum was unsure of what the future held.' Instinctively, the group leader tries to turn discussion back to what is happening in the immediate present, away from speculations about the future. This ability to move away from trouble spots in the discussions that we have in Shared Reading groups is necessary; often there are no solutions that we can offer to the differences that come up, and it would be fruitless to allow these differences to become too dominant. Yet I still feel that somehow it was a good thing that both the mum and the dad were able to become visible in their differences on this occasion. It is an instance of being able to be oneself in company, and to be seen as such, whilst at the same time being aware of another.

Shared Reading can be unifying because of the focus that the literature provides. But I also think that part of the richness of the Shared Reading experience comes from the range of individual perspectives that readers bring to the sessions. It is like realising a form of the world in miniature.

In a novel, the reader can accept that the outlook of one character will not match that of another. There is something about seeing characters in the round and often also from the inside that helps clarify that distinctiveness which makes an individual, and an individual way of seeing. If we were to imagine the dad and mum in this reading group session as if they were characters in a novel, it is quite unlikely that we should feel it necessary that their minds meet in agreement. As William Blake famously puts it: 'without contraries is no progression'. Rival forces can instead help push the narrative of life along, and bring additional dimensions to the concept we hold of the world we inhabit.

Two weeks after the vote, in a team meeting at The Reader the poem 'Revolutions' by Matthew Arnold helped us to think about the massive changes and upheavals which have determined what we know of human history. The first three verses convey something of the ongoing process:

> **Before man parted for this earthly strand,**
> **While yet upon the verge of heaven he stood,**
> **God put a heap of letters in his hand,**
> **And bade him make with them what word he could.**

And man has turn'd them many times; made Greece,
Rome, England, France; yes, nor in vain essay'd
Way after way, changes that never cease!
The letters have combined, something was made.

But ah! An inextinguishable sense
Haunts him that he has not made what he should;
That he has still, though old, to recommence,
Since he has not yet found the word God would.

We talked about how those single names – Greece, Rome, etc –
have come to represent whole systems of thought and governance,
and how they still stand for something even though the empires
themselves have fallen. We thought too about the value of the
human impulse to create, even if the result is often incomplete
or lacking. We drew comfort from the idea that the 'essay' itself is
not 'in vain'.

But we did also wonder about the cross between the individual
and the collective in this poem. In that third verse the notion of
a man grown old brings with it a sense of having been through so
much already. It is harder here to recommence than to commence.
Man, in this poem, is as an individual who has to be able to find a
way to continue to the end, rather than a succession of generations
each of whom invent their own directions to follow. There is no
one else to whom the task can be left.

It helps though to be granted this perspective from which it
feels clear that neither Greece, Rome, England nor France are the
chief aim and end; that, while we become absorbed and occupied
with the sphere in which we live and work, the point of human
existence goes beyond these different variations and embodiments
of itself.

Could the point be to discover and locate, wherever it or they
might be found, 'the good'? I do think that poem from Brendan
Kennelly with which I began does represent something of what
Shared Reading is about in this respect. Shared Reading does not
stipulate in advance who it is for. Neither does it stipulate exactly
what texts should be read, or what we should think about them.
Nevertheless, in creating a space in which to reflect on what it
is to be human, I do believe that often through Shared Reading
different forms and manifestations of 'the good' can begin to

emerge. Somehow it is possible regardless of one's affiliations or the degree to which a person might have been unable to make their own life work. Again I think this comes back to the honesty of being oneself amongst others.

Brendan Kennelly writes:

The good incline to praise,
To have the knack of seeing that
The best is not destroyed
Although forever threatened.

The good may not be 'the best', but perhaps to know that such a thing exists is to have a goodness worth protecting and celebrating. There is a confidence here too, and a belief in persistence whatever the latest threat. But the reason 'the good' are able to have this staying power is that, as here, there is a 'knack of seeing'. It is easy to get stuck without this, and I wonder if many of us do find ourselves stuck for the lack of this very 'knack'. But within such a predicament, perhaps we can allow the Poets at times to do the seeing for us. Matthew Arnold himself suggests this in his own appeal to 'thou' in the final verse of 'Revolutions':

One day, thou say'st, there will at last appear
The word, the order, which God meant should be.
Ah! We shall know that well when it comes near;
The band will quit man's heart, he will breathe free.

Admittedly, this is a hard read for one unsure of whether there can be any divinely inspired order to hope for. But let's try and be Arnold just for a moment and imagine what it would be like to take in the words of this 'thou'. I like the line: 'We shall know that well when it comes near'. 'We' stands out here after so many repetitions of 'he'. Arnold's addressee may be able to speak of the future appearance of what 'God meant', but it is 'we' who shall somehow have the gift of knowing 'it' when it arrives. It is as though at this point in the poem Arnold suddenly has the confidence to own his membership of the human race, and invites us to do the same. There is something to hope in for us, and indeed we already have it in us to know what collectively we most need.

THE READING REVOLUTION

THE UNCONQUERABLE SOUL

Angelina D'Roza

I've been facilitating Shared Reading groups for inpatient adults with acute mental health difficulties for two years, and if I were to condense the Reader's Read to Lead training into one thought, it would be that to facilitate is not to lead at all, but to carve a space, to not preempt where a story or poem might take a reader, what they might see in it, but instead to allow their response to form, to encourage and nurture that response and to pursue whatever dialogue comes from it. There seems to be a genuine willingness by people on the wards to join in with the reading group, often people who say they don't normally read, people who turn away from other group activities on the wards. So why reading?

'A book is the only place you can examine a fragile thought without breaking it, or explore an explosive idea without fear it will go off in your face' (Edward P. Morgan). If Shared Reading had a tagline, it could be this. But of course, things might go off in your face. Those fragile thoughts, those explosive ideas, come with feelings, confused and confusing. A character can identify unexpectedly with some grief, some memory, a story cut close to home. Do we turn to books for escape or explanation? I've just finished reading *H is for Hawk*, by Helen Macdonald. It's the story of her grief for her dad through the plot of training a goshawk. I haven't lost a parent but I have lost. I've cried with her, for her, for myself, enjoyed the language, the narrative, sympathised, empathised, found escape in the woods where she flew her hawk Mabel and connected with her desire to run away into the wild. It helps to know that other people feel the way you do, even in small ways, to know recovery can mean many things, and that it doesn't have to resemble some misremembered past, or the happy-ever-after. We don't have to aspire to fairy tale endings for life to be good. What a relief.

What we take away from a story or poem is a mixture of what's gone into it and the experiences we bring to the reading. Clive James says in his *Poetry Notebook*, 'So much can happen, and in such a short space, only because we bring our own history to the poem, even as it brings the poet's history to us'. What you get out of *H is for Hawk* isn't for me to say but what two or more people get out of it might *expand* through the act of sharing. Read the first stanza of W. E. Henley's 'Invictus':

> **Out of the night that covers me,**
> **Black as the pit from pole to pole,**
> **I thank whatever gods may be**
> **For my unconquerable soul.**

When I first spoke to someone about Shared Reading, she told me about a meeting she'd had and a woman who carried this poem around in her purse. The strength to be found in words is like magic. Whatever 'night' she experienced, the black 'from pole to pole' that made her keep that magic close, is unique to her, but in that meeting the poem gave her the means to express it. My nights aren't the same as hers, but her story moved me. I can repeat the final lines of this poem at my most vulnerable: 'I am the master of my fate: / I am the captain of my soul', and feel the power filling my chest. I am the captain of my soul, and to hell with you, if you doubt it. Words can do that. They did it for this woman who carried that scrap of paper in her purse, and she passed it on to my colleague, who passed it on to me. We find strength in words, but in shared words we might also find community, conversation, understanding, perhaps.

As facilitators, I think what we do well, with the ward's support, is to create the environment where that can happen. This isn't therapy, and that non-clinical status might help people to relax. We're not trying to analyse or diagnose. We haven't gone in as anything more daunting than readers. This is for fun, to pass the time, have a cup of tea. It's about communication, how we present ourselves, verbally, non-verbally, to give a sense of inclusion, safety. It's active listening structured around a Steinbeck story, for example. People seem to see an opening to say something they want to say. It might be deeply personal or not at all. There's no difference in value. Being heard is valuable.

The last session I facilitated there was a man who spent the whole story saying that it wasn't for him, that there wasn't enough action, 'no bullets'. But what he also said was a great deal about what *was* for him, what his life had been like. Even with his reservations, perhaps *because* of them, he was engaging with the story, and his engagement helped someone else in the group who was anxious and struggling to focus. For two people not really into the story, who didn't know each other, that story held them inside an imaginative and generous space for an hour. Stories have always been central to being human. They help us express ourselves and empathise with others, to escape our own skin, or see ourselves more clearly. Stories help us make connections on the page. Shared stories help us make connections in the world.

YOUR REGULARS

CLIMBING THE HILL

Ian McMillan

This is a narrative that can be distilled to the layered and echoing narratives of a folk tale, comforting and strange at the same time. Here is the man on a warm evening, climbing the hill. Here is the man in the ancient place singing for his supper. Here is the man in the darkened room, sleeping. Here is the man waking up to bars of morning gold through the curtains of the room, waking up to a new world that feels shabby and rusty and frightening and so the man reaches for a book.

June 23rd 2016; the day of the EU Referendum, and I'm doing a gig in Macclesfield with my friend the cartoonist Tony Husband at a lovely Unitarian Church down an alley in that town woven from silk. I'm looking forward to the gig because I like nothing better than showing off in public. I'm optimistic about the referendum, too, on this day of days, partly because I'm a born optimist about most things, and partly because I sense there's something in the air, something about remaining, something about wanting to gaze outwards rather than glancing in. I climb that steep hill from the station to the venue and I pass a few cheery words with some people handing out Remain stickers; as I nip into the Unitarian Church I remember that I was optimistic about the election in 2015, thinking that people would choose the future rather than the past. I was wrong.

The gig is wonderful; a packed room swaying and weeping with laughter, mascara running, inhalers being brandished and shaken. During the show I read a few poems and tell a few stories then Tony joins me and we make up a rhyming interactive cartoon show with the audience, writing the results on our flipcharts. When performances are going well, when the ideas are flowing and the laughter is gargantuan, I feel as alive as it is possible to feel. I don't feel sixty years old; I feel twenty five, or maybe twenty five and a half. At one point during the improvisation I mention a kitchen roll and the vicar of the church, from up in the balcony, completely unexpectedly hurls a kitchen roll into the space and the paper unfurls like a flag and I think, 'I am in paradise'. For a brief couple of hours the referendum has slipped my mind, like a mild backache can disappear while you sleep.

After the gig Tony drops me off at the Premier Inn in Stockport on his way home to Gee Cross; I stay here so often after gigs that it feels like my country home, my pied-a-terre, and I snore to the muted soundtrack of planes making their way down to Manchester Airport. I'm an early riser and I always enjoy the stroll at 0530 to the railway station, past the closed-down Chinese takeaway with the handwritten sign in the window that thanks people for their custom over the years. Time for bed, but first I make a cup of tea and check the news. The polling stations have closed and they're saying there will be no news for hours, so it's not going to be like an election night. I drink the tea and go to bed; it was quite an energetic gig and I fall asleep instantly, and I probably dream of flying kitchen rolls and empty takeaways.

In the middle of the night someone comes down the corridor and I hear his door bang and he wakes me up, so I turn my trusty radio on and tune in to the news. And it sounds like we're leaving. And I want to weep. For a moment I think it's later than it is, I think that sunlight is bathing the curtains with tomorrow, but actually it's just the harsh security lights that illuminate the car park like a stage set.

I reach to the bedside cupboard and pick up my book. It's a collection of poetry and prose by the great French writer Yves Bonnefoy, translated by Hoyt Rogers and published by Yale University Press. I've always loved Bonnefoy for his combination of mystery and simplicity and for his unflinching gaze on the natural world. The book falls open at a poem I've been reading a lot lately, from his sequence *A Stone*, about a past that could be so distant it meets itself coming back and locates itself firmly in the present: 'they slept and slept, distressed by the world./Memories passed through their sleep/Like boats in the fog, stoking their fires/ before they head upstream.' I think of memories passing through sleep, and I feel oddly comforted. I read on, down the poem.

'They woke, but the grass had already turned black./ Let wind be their water, and shadow their bread./ Unknowing and silence their ring./An armful of night all their fire on earth.'

The words, swimming through the mist of transformation from a language I don't understand to one that I do, make me want to read more poems in translation, make me want to reach out and connect on this awful morning, make me want to feel part of a worldwide community of writers and readers and thinkers and talkers. Let memories pass through my sleep like boats in the fog.

Then, as I sit down to write this a week or so after the referendum, I hear that Bonnefoy has died, which shocks me because I always want poets to live forever. I mourn the one voice silenced and the fact that there will be no new work from this amazing writer.

This folk tale has no neat ending. The man writes. The Premier Inn, Stockport waits for next time. But the hill up from Macclesfield Station: I'm sure that in the memory it wasn't quite this steep, this hard to climb.

UNSTABLE ELEMENT

Joseph Conrad is an exasperating writer, equally precise and diffuse. He's not exasperating on purpose however but rather in recognition of the truth of things:

> **All vessels are handled in the same way as far as theory goes, just as you may deal with all men on broad and rigid principles. But if you want that success in life which comes from the affection and confidence of your fellows, then with no two men, however similar they may appear in their nature, will you deal in the same way. There may be a rule of conduct; there is no rule of human fellowship. To deal with men is as fine an art as it is to deal with ships. Both men and ships live in an unstable element, are subject to subtle and powerful influences, and want to have their merits understood rather than their faults found out.**
>
> (*The Mirror of the Sea*)

What starts as a tart reproof to those whose method involves rules and riding roughshod ('All vessels are handled in the same way *as far as theory goes...*'), ends with that lovely and complex thought offered in a single sentence, 'Both men and ships live in an unstable element...' The awkward idea for him to get through is that 'Broad and rigid principles' *will* work, but they work by ignoring the things that matter to Conrad – those 'subtle and powerful influences' that exist beyond control: sea, weather, individual minds.

What's needed is a kind of practical faith. There may be faults but they're of no use and correcting them is a distraction. As Stein says in *Lord Jim*:

> **A man that is born falls into a dream like a man who falls into the sea. If he tries to climb out into the air as inexperienced people endeavour to do, he drowns – *nicht wahr?*... No! I tell you! The way is to the destructive element submit yourself, and with the exertions of your hands and feet in the water make the deep, deep sea keep you up.**

ONE-PAGER

YOUR REGULARS

A WAY BACK

Jane Davis

Redeemable: A memoir of darkness and hope, by Erwin James, Bloomsbury

E rwin James is a *Guardian* columnist and author, a trustee of the Prison Reform Trust and a Patron of The Reader. *Redeemable*, his memoir, builds on and expands what we know of him through his two collections of essays, *A Life Inside: A Prisoner's Notebook* and *The Home Stretch: From Prison to Parole*. Erwin is a convicted murderer who spent twenty years in prison before his release in 2004. You can read his remarkable essay on the power of reading in *The Reader* magazine, No. 54.

Though I knew it would be a sad, hard book, I had been longing to read *Redeemable*, because Erwin is a remarkable man, and because 'How do people change?' has been one of my key obsessions for thirty years. As I write these life-size numbers – twenty years, thirty years – I feel both how long and how short are these lives I am reading and thinking about.

I read the book over three days, nights and early mornings this week. The first reading session gave me nightmares. That's not a very comfortable recommendation for a book, but don't be put off. There are particular reasons why I would be moved to nightmares by Erwin's story. The remorselessly crazy helter-

the reader no.54

ESSAY

WHERE A GOOD BOOK MIGHT TAKE YOU

Erwin James

*To assume you exist on dreams', nightmares and desires
by Justice Secretary Chris Grayling, means that UK prisoners
from receiving books and other items in the post. Try and to
prisoners is inevitably demoralising. Guardian columnist Erwin Ja
writes about the profound effect our book had on his time in prison,
every year sentence.*

*see newly launched blog to read our list of recommended reads from
ers,* **www.thereadermagazine.co.uk**

...o you exist on dreams, nightmares and desires
...u are locked and isolated in a cell for twenty three
... of twenty four hour you try to block the realities
...dreams and occasionally, indulge in fantas...
...n after I was sentenced to life impriso...
...Old Bailey to Wandsworth prison it was
...quent skills, or abilities and almost that
...overcome my prospects were bleak. It wa
...to rationalise my situation - to see what
...personal development. But first with
...found that I lacked even the desire to
...I had become – little more that a...
...The early weeks and months of my
...that a life spent in prison could
...destructive.

DREYFUS'S PRISON

by Martin Argles
Guardian photographer

skelter of a family dominated by unacknowledged pain, dogged by poverty, and knocked about by hunger and alcohol brought alive many memories of my own childhood. And for all the brute reality of memory and fact, there's something blank, which I found as frightening as anything else, this blank numbness, recalling William Empson's poem, 'Let It Go';

It is this deep blankness is the real thing strange.
The more things happen to you the more you can't
Tell or remember even what they were.

The contradictions cover such a range.
The talk would talk and go so far aslant.
You don't want madhouse and the whole thing there.

It is as if, even now, after all this thinking and sifting and remembering, Erwin cannot fathom his father, whom he loved, loved, loved. But why, after his wife's death, did Erwin Snr continually abandon his children? Why did he beat his little son? It's as if Erwin has, in the end, simply to let it go, 'the contradictions cover such a range'. There are no answers and no time for answers in the first two-thirds of the book, which feels a rushing headlong descent towards the newspaper clipping that gives the bare, public details of Erwin's trial for double murder.

Erwin mentions reading *Crime and Punishment* in prison many years later, and I felt as I read that the world of *Redeemable* was lit by the same feverish pained misery as Dostoevsky's novel. So, as a twelve-year-old, Erwin is living in a children's home when he gets into a fight at school and runs away, from Ilkley to Shipley, an eight mile walk, to the place he thinks his father is living. His father's girlfriend won't let him stay and sends him on to Aunt Bridie's house:

She told me where my aunt Bridie's house was and said that Maw (Erwin's much loved grandmother) was staying with her and my uncle Jake. Bursting with excitement I sped off to find them. The house was at the top of the estate, the very roughest part where houses had windows missing and holes in front doors. When I arrived I banged on the door as loud as I could.

As soon as she saw me Aunt Bridie threw her arms around me and hugged me tight. 'Maw, look,' she called to the living room. 'It's wee Erwin!'

I cried with joy when I saw Maw and rushed to her, grabbing hold of her and sobbing into her arms. 'Oh, son,' she said, 'look at the size of you!' I hadn't seen her since a few weeks after the crash (in which Erwin's mother was killed) more than five years earlier. She looked very old and not at all well. She had a great blue and black bruise on the left side of her face. 'Don't worry son,' she said when I stared. 'I just fell doon the stairs when I was tired.' I could smell alcohol on her breath. Around the room I saw empty beer and wine bottles and realised that Maw, Aunt Bridie and Uncle Jake were all drunk.

The police picked me up in Shipley town centre two days later and after a couple of hours in the police station I was taken back to the Home.

And so it goes on, the unstoppable blur of drunken faces, robberies and runnings-off that make up this child-and-early-adulthood.

At one point in the week, *Redeemable* is in my mind as I watch a young mother playing with her three-month-old baby. The mother is holding the baby about ten inches away from her face, completely focusing the child's attention. The mother smiles and talks, nodding, making deep contact. 'Aren't you a lovely one, you are, aren't you?' She pauses, waits patiently, holds the child, and continues to nod and smile. In response, the baby smiles and coos, almost, you'd say, speaks back. They talk to one another, communing, communicating for ten, fifteen minutes as I watch. I'm thinking of Wordsworth's *Prelude* where in Book 2, the babe 'nursed in his mother's arms… doth gather passion from his mother's eye.' Wordsworth observed, as psychologists and baby-watchers have done, that the baby recognises its feelings in the faces of others, and gradually learns through language to name those feelings. Language is what we use to communicate between inside our wordless, feeling-driven selves and the outside world of everyone else. Language is what we have to help us become part of humanity; language and role-models, as William Blake knew. His poems 'Infant Joy' and 'Infant Sorrow' give us the psychology in two tiny nutshells.

Erwin, like many children who fall into the Care system and later into prison, doesn't have much in the way of role-models (though he loves reading and writing and – a school failure – loves English). He learns what his family teaches him: to love without hope of love returned, to drink as a way to escape the pain of being unbeloved, and to hurt others as he has been hurt. Care teaches him nothing but that he is a criminal. It is only when he is convicted and meets the patient, one might even say loving, psychologist, Joan Branton, that you feel the human exchange, the eye contact, the focus, the shared language of feelings begin to enter his consciousness. He is no baby: he is twenty–eight years old.

But Joan gives him time, conversation, books, including *Crime and Punishment*. 'What have you done to yourself?' Sonia the prostitute asks Raskolnikov the murderer in one of that novel's culminating moments. This is one of the questions Joan invites Erwin to consider.

The book is testimony to the possibility of redemption, to the work of some of those working in the prison system and to Erwin James' creation for himself of an inner life, a set of values, and a belief, learned from Joan, that we are redeemable. 'There is always a way back,' she tells him, 'if you want it badly enough and are prepared to work hard enough.'

Highly recommended, but it is a hard read. Have tissues and time to recover. Then send some books to prisoners or support the work of The Reader in prisons and other criminal justice settings.

'Honest and compelling' Martina Cole

'Truly incredible' Larry Lamb

Redeemable

A Memoir of Darkness and Hope

Erwin James

'Heartbreaking, poignant and affecting'
Stephen Kelman

BLOOMSBURY CIRCUS

YOUR REGULARS

WHAT IT TAKES

Enid Stubin

Cruising down Third Avenue, I see outside the Vintage Thrift Shop a little desk marked '$25—Must go before end of day' and think of my student Huan, here from Chengdu and thrilled to learn that we're in the secondhand center of New York City. Huan and her classmates arrived a month ago and already we've had two weeks of English 2100T, freshman writing for English-as-Second Language college students. They're looking for apartments and meeting roommates and learning the subway system, organizing weekend outings to Rockaway (although my friend Gwen and Sandra, the one student from Ukraine, insist that Brighton is the beach to beat). They were excited to learn about the half-dozen secondhand shops all within a two-block radius of Baruch College, a world of buyables from Housing Works and the New York City Opera thrift shops to the Salvation Army and Paws for Cause. When out-of-towners visit, these are the landmarks I lead them to, and my students from southwest China and Ukraine need to know where to find inexpensive kitchenware and serviceable furniture.

I translate the slippery term *vintage*, both denotation and connotation, and provide the term my student Thierno uses, *des fripperies*, for the used clothing and housewares much prized in Guinea. When he passed his writing exam, which had loomed as an almost insurmountable obstacle, we celebrated at Housing Works, where Thierno found himself a dashing Dolce and Gabbana jumper for $8. Although I cited the law that forbids New York City employees from accepting gifts, he insisted on presenting me with a $3 green glass dish that he saw me admire. Don't tell the City University brass—I accepted it.

I was told that my international students were strong in English skills, and I'm pretty casual about the design of a course. I like the accidental approach of unfurling the *New York Times* and fixing on an article, but the Baruch bookstore was having trouble arranging for the reduced-price subscriptions. Tucked into my bag was a copy of *The Long-Winded Lady*, a collection of essays by Maeve Brennan that had appeared in *The New Yorker* from 1953-1968. In 'From the Hotel Earle,' the narrator settles herself and her cats into her customary room, then sallies forth in Greenwich Village to choose books, to buy herself a flower for her lapel, anticipate a leisurely dinner out and order a drink. Waiting for dessert, she refuses to believe that a young woman has suddenly, arbitrarily, incomprehensibly died. '"But she's not dead," I said.' The specificity of the narrator's choices—Benedict Kiely and Patricia Highsmith, carnation, University Restaurant, martini, coffee ice cream—juxtaposes the easy certainty of the ordinary and then, in the face of grief, devolves at first to anodyne and plummets down to desolation:

I hoped the woman who died on the street had had a nice day. I don't know what I didn't hope for her. I hoped she had no one belonging to her who loved her enough to grieve for years, to cry all their lives over the thought of her lying there like that.

Having encountered the essay after the sudden and impossible death of a young colleague, I'd already been dazzled by its poignancy and grit, Brennan's balancing of the straightforward and the transcendent. Offering it to my students for a first reading and writing assignment, I hoped to learn something about them, because Brennan like them was a transplant to the city, and their sympathetic interpretations did not disappoint.

In another essay, 'The Good Adano', the narrator is tart—acidulous, really. Relieved to find a favorite restaurant open on an oppressively hot and humid Fourth of July weekend, just like the summer we were having, she sneers at two customers, 'tall, strong, opulently shaped girls of about thirty who looked as though they must be in show business' and dressed in 'slinky, skintight, slithering dresses that recalled the body of Circe, the gestures of Salome, and the intentions of Aphrodite'. Carrying 'cloudy' fur stoles and 'fat little handbag[s]', they commit the cardinal sin of consuming 'big plates of hot soup, plates piled with meat and vegetables, and plates with heaps of salad, and they ate a lot of crusty Adano bread with butter, and when all that was gone they had coffee—American coffee—and a slice each of glistening rum cake'. The narrator is

deeply fascinated by them, because their closed faces and their positive, concentrated gestures excluded every single thing in the world except themselves.

My student Sandra, who works five and six days a week at a high-end German version of a British pub in Tribeca, was impatient with the narrator's stance: 'First of all, they're tourists, and they packed the wrong clothes, because it was cold where they come from and because you want to wear pretty, fancy clothes in the big city. And they eat—but what does the narrator eat? She only orders martini'. I loved Sandra's impious take, coming as it did from her own observational gifts honed in the hospitality trade.

Trawling the internet, Rachel found photos of Brennan from the 1948: beautiful and imperially slim, dressed exquisitely in meticulously tailored black and precisely chosen accessories, looking at once anachronistic and perfectly reflective of her time. Her biography by Angela Bourke, subtitled *Homesick at The New Yorker* and sub-subtitled *An Irish in Exile*, reminds us that she allowed herself only two hard-boiled eggs a day while working on an article. Internet rumors posing as literary criticism suggest that Truman Capote based his Holly Golightly on Brennan; someone must have gotten around to telling Audrey Hepburn and Hubert de Givenchy about her as well.

In a letter to William Maxwell, her beloved editor at *The New Yorker* and friend, Brennan summoned up the ambivalent and troubled debt to her mother in agonized recognition and gratitude: 'P.S. She gave me everything, and now she has given me the city.' The city she intends is Dublin, the setting for Brennan's savage and luminous stories collected in *The Rose Garden* and *The*

Springs of Affection, but her merciless and compassionate gaze also considers New York. I suppose those early assignments, before the *New York Times* subscriptions kicked in, were intended as offerings: the Manhattan presented through Brennan's persona of the *Long-Winded Lady* is the city we're living in today, mediated by a woman who calls herself a 'traveler in residence'. 'That would be you,' I tell them when we meet in our high-tech classroom for four hours a day, my intrepid students who have uprooted themselves from Beijing and Chengdu and Kiev, who write of their parents— few have siblings—with open-hearted and profound gratefulness for their sacrifice and support.

This is the city I should like to give my students. Although many of Brennan's landmarks and touchstones were gone by the time I got to the city, due largely to the real-estate encroachment of New York University, I too was able to buy paperbacks and stationery at the Eighth Street Bookstore and the Village Smoke Shop. After a seedy period in the seventies and eighties, the Hotel Earle, bought by the Paul family, now caters to a largely international crowd as the Washington Square Hotel; I consider its dining room, North Square, one of my clubs, where Chad and Ryan and Jordana embody the spirit of hospitality and affection.

So let me give you Maya, who writes on the last day of class:

I live at 126 MacDougal Street. I guess the reason why I am so enchanted with it is that this place has an atmosphere of vitality. The restaurant with blue-white desks and white daisy in glass bottles reminds me of ocean. The old red apartments are telling the old fairy tales like a grandmother. Every evening when I get to home, I sit near the window and appreciate the sunset glow for a long time—purple, red, blue, white, grey. Have I lived there for two months?

Ariel, who calls herself a 'nerdy idealist', wonders '"What did this city tell you in the past month?" Well, I guess there is no better answer than "Welcome to the real world."' And Alina writes of her new home, 'It's a place of opportunity and challenge; but it is easy for you to feel lonely... Still, my classmates and teachers made me feel that I will never be alone in this city. I think I will begin to fall in love with this city.'

I think so too.

YOUR REGULARS

ASK THE READER

Brian Nellist

Q In Tolstoy and Turgenev gentry and peasants talk to each other with a frankness and honesty for which I can't think of any equivalent in their English contemporaries. Is the submissiveness and sometimes the absence of servants in English writing a sign of social guilt?

A To be frank, no, it isn't, because they are not absent and rarely submissive, though it's an interesting issue. Historically, in the Medieval and Early Modern romances the place of the servant is occupied by page and squire and in the book that is the source and origin of the European novel, *Don Quixote*, the major part of the book consists of the conversations of the Don and his attendant, Sancho Panza. The exalted literary speech of Quixote is challenged by his literal-minded and pragmatic retainer. But it is also more complicated than that because the master can use the threat of enchantment to explain away apparent delusion quite rationally and his page takes the game seriously because though they are both poor men, Sancho serves for the sake of making his fortune. They often change places, as it were. In English the greatness of Cervantes, the other quater-centenarian of course, is simplified but this model he initiated is observable I suppose in Crusoe and Friday, Tom Jones and Partridge, Squire Bramble and Humphry Clinker and with many variations in Walter Scott. In *Pamela* because the servant is a woman the idea is sexualised. The relationship is recognisable in many different forms in Sherlock Holmes and Watson, for example, in Wooster and Jeeves, in Morecambe and Wise, etc, etc...

But it's in the Victorian period that the relationship becomes especially interesting. Sam Weller, for example, because he is street-wise and a humourist chooses to become a servant to Pickwick when he sets out on his travels because he recognises his master's innocence and gullibility, expects adventures but sees himself as protector. Or, again, Mark Tapley, wanting to test his irrefragable cheerfulness, engages his services to young Chuzzlewit precisely because he tests himself through his master's blithe selfishness and unthinking optimism. Dickens also observes the increasing specialisation of the servant role in his society so he has an extensive repertoire of dress-makers, seamstresses, small clerks and seedy shop-keepers that could have no place in Tolstoy. The peasant is tied for life to his master in the Russian novel and the unbridgeable social gulf produces, paradoxically, a freedom of exchange where in English the relationship has to be negotiated, as in Cervantes. Bob Cratchit scarcely speaks to Scrooge except in brief reply but is certainly vocal in his own home over his Christmas dinner.

But this is man to man stuff whereas the more interesting issues arise over the situation of women in service, including the slight suggestiveness of that phrase. When *Anna Karenina* opens with a governess being dismissed because of Stiva Oblonksy's affair we do not hear her side of the story. But partly because so many great Victorian novelists were women that particular role is important. The governess is essentially a servant yet by education and origin often she belongs to the same social class as her employers. Gwendolen in *Daniel Deronda* feels herself forced into marriage with a man who has degraded another woman, to avoid assuming the responsibility for the children of a bishop's wife whom she finds conventionally vulgar. Jane Eyre finds herself being employed by another woman, a housekeeper, with the charge of the daughter of an absent father. As herself a servant she consistently addresses Rochester as 'Sir' right up to the altar (for the second time). The feeling of oppression dominates Anne Brönte's Agnes Gray and she finds release only through marriage to a curate, himself of course a kind of underling. Readers who too easily ascribe the treatment of Hetty in *Adam Bede* to George Eliot's supposed dislike of beautiful woman totally miss the point. Beauty is this dairy-maid's supreme asset, the source of her dreams of escape into a more fulfilling world but the fantasy of fine dresses and bright ballrooms destroys instead of liberating her. To put it cynically, she was not as clever as Samuel Richardson's Pamela.

But since in your question you mention talking 'freely', the established woman servant can also speak with a kind of independence of mind secured by the privilege of her sex. When Ellen Dean in *Wuthering Heights* is rebuked by Edgar Linton who has found his wife in delirium after Heathcliff's tirade, she doesn't accept it meekly:

I performed the duty of a faithful servant in telling you, and I have got a faithful servant's wages! Well, it will teach me to be careful next time. Next time you may gather intelligence for yourself.

The metaphor of 'wages' and resentment over them display self-confidence but also an acknowledgement that attendants in a household become a kind of spy; indeed the testimony of servants was often used in the rare contemporary divorce cases. In small households the single female helper of a certain age, part of the house yet not of the family becomes a kind of honorary aunt. In Mrs Gaskell's 'Half a Lifetime Ago' when Susan Dixon dismisses her fiancé in order to save her mentally disturbed brother from being put into an asylum, it's the servant who confirms her choice; "'Lass!' said Peggy, solemnly, "thou hast done well."' The 'solemnly' comes as a kind of benediction, with authority. In the short novel *Cousin Phillis* when the daughter of the close-knit and devout family falls passionately in love with a man who goes abroad and marries there, she becomes desperately ill. It's the family servant who understands it all, better than the family and speaks her mind:

'We ha' done a' we can, and the doctors has done a' they can for you, and I think the Lord has done a' He can for you, and more than you deserve, too, if you don't do something for yourself.

She understands better than anyone how destructively self-absorbing the grief has become; 'Fight your own way back to cheerfulness'. The 'we' is significant ('We ha' done a' we can'); she's a part of the family but she sees more than the mother and father because she also is not. I've been tempted by your generalisation into my own but the circumstances have the particularity that is the strength of the novel and resist such attempts at system.

THE NEGLECTED NOVEL

MARK RUTHERFORD 'MICHAEL TREVANION'

Brian Nellist

William Hale White (Mark Rutherford), 1831–1913, *Miriam's Schooling* (1890), 'Michael Trevanion'

What sympathy can we bring to people who have given their lives for now-discredited causes? Surely the fervour, the intensity of mind inspired by their beliefs, the self-giving involved, cannot be simply dismissed as merely a mistake? It's as though the response was greater than the reasons that gave rise to it. The purely human fact outweighs the fragility of the political, economic, sexual or, as here, religious hopes involved in it. Mark Rutherford wrote six books of stories between 1881 and 1896 and *Miriam's Schooling* is the most neglected of the series. 'Michael Trevanion' is a brief novella in that volume. Michael is a strict Calvinist who believes that only the worship of the Elect is valid before God. Hale White had been dismissed from his theological college because he doubted the truth of that doctrine and resisted the notion that every word of the Bible was directly inspired by the Holy Ghost. All his novels spring in one way or another from his denial of such exclusiveness. They are not really accounts of actions but meditations on the mental processes behind them. As a young man Hale White had been George Eliot's assistant at the *Westminster Review* and his brief tales are in a way a response to her work.

This is a story about a father and his son. Michael as a youngster married, passionately, a woman who turned out to have little understanding of his ideas and all his deeply emotional nature therefore is devoted to his child Robert. But Robert has fallen in love with the local beauty who lives in their little Cornish town and whom he's saved from drowning. She belongs, this is the terrible issue, to a conventional church-going family, evidently not among the Elect. The father 'loved his son with a father's love but with a mother's too... There was in him also that wild ferocious passion', as though he had given birth to him. Robert inherits all the devotion that Michael cannot give to his tepid wife and daughter. Yet he doesn't quite understand that son either:

> **Robert was inconsistent, as the old doctrine when it is decaying, or the new at its advent always is; but the main difference between Michael and Robert was not any distinct divergence, but that truths believed by Michael, and admitted by Robert, failed to impress Robert with that depth and sharpness of cut with which they were wrought into his father. Mere assent is nothing; the question of importance is whether the figuration of the creed is dull or vivid – as vivid as the shadows of a June sun on a white house.**

Robert works for his father as a builder and so, in Cornwall, also a stone-mason. Michael we are told was 'considered something of a fossil', something, that is, in this case deeply embedded in the rock itself. The figuration could be an ammonite or ancient bone but to Robert the shape of things has been replaced by a feeling, a mere 'assent'.

For Michael therefore the issue is not whether his son should be temporarily happy but that his soul should be saved for all eternity. For the sake of that he is willing to commit what he believes to be a great evil knowing that he himself will be damned for it by a just God so long as Robert is saved. Yet behind the intensity of that choice the book recognises ordinary pressures unacknowledged by

Michael himself. How terrible for parents when they realise 'that the deepest secrets in their children are entrusted not to them but to others'. He sees Robert, he thinks, making the same mistake in his marriage as he had made himself. If as reader you want to protest against the singularity of belief responsible for such pain the book itself will support you:

> **We complain of people because they are not original, but we do not ask what their originality, if they had any, would be worth. Better a thousand times than the originality of most of us is the average common-sense which is not our own exclusively, but shared with millions of our fellow-beings, and is not due to any one of them.**

We do not take Michael seriously if we regard him merely aesthetically as an interesting eccentric. Better than that, lacking Trevanion's belief, to settle for the ordinary gumption that is our common birthright.

I'm not going even to hint at what happens; you must read it for yourself. Suffice it to say that it is, despite all misgivings the glory of Michael that he does not act or think in the way most of us do. The fossils remind us of a world we have lost but they remind us that somewhere buried in our ancestral consciousness, like the rock, we have been there and been him.

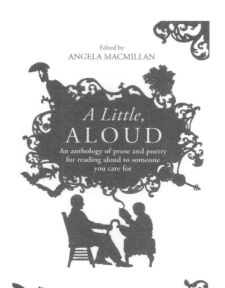

'Being read to is the beguiling beginning of learning to love reading – it opens the door to absolutely everything and anything we might want to do in life.'

Joanna Trollope

'Reading aloud is one of the paths to greater happiness in life. It's pleasure. Pure pleasure.'

Stephen Fry

£12.99 RRP

(including p&p if bought online from www.thereader.org.uk)

Minted: Practical Poetry for Life, edited by Brian Nellist

To buy, please send a cheque for £5 to The Reader:

The Reader (Minted), Calderstones Mansion House, Calderstones Park, Liverpool, L18 3JB
See www.thereader.org.uk for more details

FEATURING FIVE

Angela Macmillan

Chris Packham, *Fingers in the Sparkle Jar*
Ebury, Random House, (2016) ISBN-13: 978-1785033483

This is definitely not your standard celebrity autobiography. Chris Packham recalls his boyhood from seven to sixteen in astonishingly vivid, poetic prose. Wildlife fascinated him from the start: tadpoles tasted, ladybirds jam-jarred and birds eggs blown. His long-suffering parents, already involved in their own marital problems, acknowledged their son's passion and allowed him the freedom to explore. The sheer strength of his passion and his obsessive nature meant he would focus on his current preoccupation, be it otters or foxes or dinosaurs to the exclusion of everything else. He found and trained a kestrel; it became his whole world so that he was catastrophically traumatised when it died. It was not until he was an adult and outside the book's timespan that Asperger's was diagnosed. In adolescence his separating 'difference' became more prominent and schooldays were a misery of isolation. Depression nearly ended in tragedy and the memoir is interspersed with much later conversations with his psychiatrist. However his Asperger's also provided him with positive opportunities: the ability to see things with intensity, to record them and systemise them and to be able to recall them with equal and sparkling intensity. This is a remarkable and brilliantly original book.

Margaret Laurence, *The Fire-Dwellers* (1988)

In her novel, *A Jest of God*, Margaret Laurence writes of Rachel, a lonely spinster living in a small Canadian town with her mother. *The Fire-Dwellers* tells the story of Rachel's sister Stacey who, in spite of being married with four children, is conscious of being 'alone in a houseful of people'. We listen to her interior monologue made up of memories, her current frustration with motherhood and interspersed with headlines from the media and conversations with God and her neighbours. Stacey drinks too much, often behaves badly and always regrets: 'nothing is ever looked at and torn up and thrown away like scrap paper. The abrasions just go on accumulating. What a lot of heavy invisible garbage we live with.' Part confession, part spiritual exploration, this is an impressive novel and disgracefully out of print in the UK.

Hans Fallada, *Alone in Berlin* (1947)
Penguin Classics (2010) ISBN-13: 978-0141189383

Otto Quangel, a shop foreman, waits for his wife to open a letter from their son who is serving at the front. 'In his quiet undemonstrative way, he loves this woman very much'. It is as well to remember this early fragment for there is nothing else remotely warm about Otto and practically nothing to alleviate the darkness and sinister atmosphere of fear in 1940s Berlin. It was a time when shortages meant meagre existence, neighbour informed on neighbour and to act in any way against The Party meant imprisonment. The letter informs him of the death of his son and Otto is shocked into a decision to resist. Slowly and painstakingly he and his wife write anti-Nazi slogans on postcards which they drop across the city. The cards are pathetic and ineffectual but the act of defiance is mighty. When the Gestapo Inspector Escherich becomes obsessed with solving the case, the tension becomes almost unbearable and discovery inevitable. The ending is a long slow descent into the hell of underground prison cells where flashes of courage and human decency resist the final horror. Fallada could have left Berlin but stayed and bore witness.

Martha Gellhorn, *A Stricken Field* (1942)
University of Chicago Press (2011) ISBN-13: 978-0226286969

Martha Gellhorn, briefly married to Ernest Hemingway, was a war correspondent during the 1930s. This, her first full-length novel, calls on her professional experience in Prague in 1938 following the Munich Agreement. Jewish and communist refugees who had fled the Sudetenland and come to Czechoslovakia were now being forced to return to certain imprisonment and death in concentration camps. In the novel, Mary Douglas, an American journalist, finds she is powerless to help her Jewish friend Rita. Written in 1940, before she knew the outcome of the war, this is a convincing and haunting account of the bravery of people living under advancing oppression. In the afterword, dated 1985, Martha Gellhorn says 'I wrote out the accumulated rage and grief of the past two years in this one story, one small aspect of the ignoble history of our time.'

Walter Kempowski, *All For Nothing* (2006)
Granta Books (2016) ISBN-13: 978-1847087218

"The Georgenhof estate was not far from Mitkau, a small town in East Prussia, and now, in winter, the Georgenhof, surrounded by old oaks, lay in a landscape like a black island in a white sea.' So begins this powerful story set at the end of 1945 as the Russians advance and the Third Reich collapses. In the estate's manor house live the von Globig family. Eberhard is serving in Italy. His reclusive wife, Katharina, 'a languorous beauty' inhabits a world of her own. Their son, twelve-year-old Peter, has managed to avoid the Hitler Youth and is casually looked after mainly by Auntie together with two Ukranian maids and a Polish overseer. The war has so far remained in the background of their lives but when Katherina hides a Jewish refugee, their flimsy sanctuary is broken and the pace of the novel gathers a terrible momentum. Kempowski's tone is coolly dispassionate. He frequently changes point of view so that we hear from all the characters, none of whom are wholly likeable or wholly unsympathetic. Today we are used to looking at war from a safe distance. The novel forces the question, what would I do, how would I behave, if it threatened *my* home?

Edited by
ANGELA MACMILLAN

A Little,
ALOUD
with Love

Prose and poetry for
reading aloud to someone
you love

A LITTLE *MORE* ALOUD

JONATHAN SWIFT

GULLIVER'S TRAVELS

Selected by Angela Macmillan

Following a shipwreck, Gulliver manages to get to shore but finds himself the sole survivor.

When I awaked, it was just day-light. I attempted to rise, but was not able to stir: for, as I happened to lie on my back, I found my arms and legs were strongly fastened on each side to the ground; and my hair, which was long and thick, tied down in the same manner. I likewise felt several slender ligatures across my body, from my arm-pits to my thighs. I could only look upwards; the sun began to grow hot, and the light offended my eyes. I heard a confused noise about me; but in the posture I lay, could see nothing except the sky. In a little time I felt something alive moving on my left leg, which advancing gently forward over my breast, came almost up to my chin; when, bending my eyes downwards as much as I could, I perceived it to be a human creature not six inches high, with a bow and arrow in his hands, and a quiver at his back. In the mean time, I felt at least forty more of the same kind (as I conjectured) following the first. I was in the utmost astonishment, and roared so loud, that they all ran back in a fright; and some of them, as I was afterwards told, were hurt with the falls they got by leaping from my sides upon the ground. However, they soon returned, and one of them, who ventured so far as to get a full sight of my face, lifting up his hands and eyes by way of admiration, cried out in a shrill but distinct voice, HEKINAH DEGUL: the others repeated the same words several times, but then I knew not what they meant. I lay all this while, as the reader may believe, in great uneasiness. At length, struggling to get loose, I had the fortune to break the strings, and wrench out the pegs that fastened my left arm to the ground; for, by lifting it up to my face, I discovered the methods they had taken to bind me, and at the same time with a violent pull, which gave me excessive pain, I a little loosened the strings that tied down my hair on the left side, so that I was just able to turn my head about two inches. But the creatures ran off a second time, before I could seize them; whereupon there was a great shout in a very shrill accent, and after it ceased I heard one of them cry aloud TOLGO PHONAC; when in an instant I felt above a hundred arrows discharged on my left hand, which, pricked me like so many needles; and besides, they shot another flight into the air, as we do bombs in Europe, whereof many, I suppose, fell on my body, (though I felt them not), and some on my face, which I immediately covered with my left hand. When this shower of arrows was over, I fell a groaning with grief and pain; and then striving again to get loose, they discharged another volley larger than the first, and some of them attempted with spears to stick me in the sides; but by good luck I had on a buff jerkin, which they could not pierce. I thought it the most prudent method to lie still, and my design was to continue so till night, when, my left hand being already loose, I could easily free myself: and as for the inhabitants, I had reason to believe I might be a match for the greatest army they could bring against me, if they were all of the same size with him that I saw. But fortune disposed otherwise of me. When the people observed I was quiet, they discharged no more arrows; but, by the noise I heard, I knew their numbers increased; and about four yards from me, over against my right ear, I heard a knocking for above an hour, like that of people at work; when turning my head that way, as well as the pegs and strings would permit me, I saw a stage erected about a foot and a half from the ground, capable of holding four of the inhabitants, with two or three ladders to mount it: from whence one of them, who seemed to be a person of quality, made me a long speech, whereof I understood not one syllable. But I should have mentioned, that before the principal person began his oration, he cried out three times, LANGRO DEHUL SAN (these words and the former were afterwards repeated and explained to me); whereupon, immediately, about fifty of the inhabitants came and cut the strings that fastened the left side of my head, which gave me the liberty of turning it to the right, and of observing the person and gesture of him that was to speak.

He appeared to be of a middle age, and taller than any of the other three who attended him, whereof one was a page that held up his train, and seemed to be somewhat longer than my middle finger; the other two stood one on each side to support him. He acted every part of an orator, and I could observe many periods of threatenings, and others of promises, pity, and kindness. I answered in a few words, but in the most submissive manner, lifting up my left hand, and both my eyes to the sun, as calling him for a witness; and being almost famished with hunger, having not eaten a morsel for some hours before I left the ship, I found the demands of nature so strong upon me, that I could not forbear showing my impatience (perhaps against the strict rules of decency) by putting my finger frequently to my mouth, to signify that I wanted food. The HURGO (for so they call a great lord, as I afterwards learnt) understood me very well. He descended from the stage, and commanded that several ladders should be applied to my sides, on which above a hundred of the inhabitants mounted and walked towards my mouth, laden with baskets full of meat, which had been provided and sent thither by the king's orders, upon the first intelligence he received of me. I observed there was the flesh of several animals, but could not distinguish them by the taste. There were shoulders, legs, and loins, shaped like those of mutton, and very well dressed, but smaller than the wings of a lark. I ate them by two or three at a mouthful, and took three loaves at a time, about the bigness of musket bullets.

They supplied me as fast as they could, showing a thousand marks of wonder and astonishment at my bulk and appetite.

FICTION

THE OLD STORY

RUDYARD KIPLING 'THE MIRACLE OF PURUN BHAGAT'

Selected by Brian Nellist

Rudyard Kipling (1865–1932)
The Second Jungle Book (1895)
'The Miracle of Purun Bhagat'

When a young man, Kipling worked as a journalist in Lahore and Allahabad so many of his early tales are set in Muslim India. Here, however, he honours the ascetic mysticism of the Hindu tradition but also its intense sympathy with animal creation and the duality of the natural world, both tender and threatening. Like the Lama in Kim, *in the end Purun returns to action.*

There was once a man in India who was Prime Minister of one of the semi-independent native States in the north-western part of the country. He was a Brahmin, so high-caste that caste ceased to have any particular meaning for him; and his father had been an important official in the gay-coloured tag-rag and bobtail of an old-fashioned Hindu Court. But as Purun Dass grew up he felt that the old order of things was changing, and that if any one wished to get on in the world he must stand well with the English, and imitate all that the English believed to be good. At the same time a native official must keep his own master's favour. This was a difficult game, but the quiet, close-mouthed young Brahmin, helped by a good English education at a Bombay University, played it coolly, and rose, step by step, to be Prime Minister of the kingdom. That is to say, he held more real power than his master the Maharajah.

When the old king – who was suspicious of the English, their railways and telegraphs – died, Purun Dass stood high with his young successor, who had been tutored by an Englishman; and between them, though he always took care that his master should have the credit, they established schools for little girls, made roads, and started State dispensaries and shows of agricultural implements, and published a yearly blue-book on the 'Moral and Material Progress of the State,' and the Foreign Office and the Government of India were delighted. Very few native States take up English progress altogether, for they will not believe, as Purun Dass showed he did, that what was good for the Englishman must be twice as good for the Asiatic. The Prime Minister became the honoured friend of Viceroys, and Governors, and Lieutenant–Governors, and medical missionaries, and common missionaries, and hard-riding English officers who came to shoot in the State preserves, as well as of whole hosts of tourists who travelled up and down India in the cold weather, showing how things ought to be managed. In his spare time he would endow scholarships for the study of medicine and manufactures on strictly English lines, and write letters to the *Pioneer*, the greatest Indian daily paper, explaining his master's aims and objects.

At last he went to England on a visit, and had to pay enormous sums to the priests when he came back; for even so high-caste a Brahmin as Purun Dass lost caste by crossing the black sea. In London he met and talked with every one worth knowing – men whose names go all over the world – and saw a great deal more than he said. He was given honorary degrees by learned universities, and he made speeches and talked of Hindu social reform to English ladies in evening dress, till all London cried, "This is the most fascinating man we have ever met at dinner since cloths were first laid."

When he returned to India there was a blaze of glory, for the Viceroy himself made a special visit to confer upon the Maharajah the Grand Cross of the Star of India – all diamonds and ribbons and enamel; and at the same ceremony, while the cannon boomed,

Purun Dass was made a Knight Commander of the Order of the Indian Empire; so that his name stood Sir Purun Dass, K.C.I.E.

That evening, at dinner in the big Viceregal tent, he stood up with the badge and the collar of the Order on his breast, and replying to the toast of his master's health, made a speech few Englishmen could have bettered.

Next month, when the city had returned to its sun-baked quiet, he did a thing no Englishman would have dreamed of doing; for, so far as the world's affairs went, he died. The jewelled order of his knighthood went back to the Indian Government, and a new Prime Minister was appointed to the charge of affairs, and a great game of General Post began in all the subordinate appointments. The priests knew what had happened, and the people guessed; but India is the one place in the world where a man can do as he pleases and nobody asks why; and the fact that Dewan Sir Purun Dass, K.C.I.E., had resigned position, palace, and power, and taken up the begging-bowl and ochre-coloured dress of a Sunnyasi, or holy man, was considered nothing extraordinary. He had been, as the Old Law recommends, twenty years a youth, twenty years a fighter – though he had never carried a weapon in his life – and twenty years head of a household. He had used his wealth and his power for what he knew both to be worth; he had taken honour when it came his way; he had seen men and cities far and near, and men and cities had stood up and honoured him. Now he would let those things go, as a man drops the cloak he no longer needs.

Behind him, as he walked through the city gates, an antelope skin and brass-handled crutch under his arm, and a begging-bowl of polished brown *coco-de-mer* in his hand, barefoot, alone, with eyes cast on the ground – behind him they were firing salutes from the bastions in honour of his happy successor. Purun Dass nodded. All that life was ended; and he bore it no more ill-will or good-will than a man bears to a colourless dream of the night. He was a Sunnyasi – a houseless, wandering mendicant, depending on his neighbours for his daily bread; and so long as there is a morsel to divide in India, neither priest nor beggar starves. He had never in his life tasted meat, and very seldom eaten even fish. A five-pound note would have covered his personal expenses for food through any one of the many years in which he had been absolute master of millions of money. Even when he was being lionised in London he had held before him his dream of peace and quiet – the long, white, dusty Indian road, printed all over with bare feet, the incessant, slow-moving traffic, and the sharp-smelling wood smoke curling up under the fig-trees in the twilight, where the wayfarers sit at their evening meal.

When the time came to make that dream true the Prime Minister took the proper steps, and in three days you might more easily have found a bubble in the trough of the long Atlantic seas, than Purun Dass among the roving, gathering, separating millions of India.

At night his antelope skin was spread where the darkness overtook him – sometimes in a Sunnyasi monastery by the roadside; sometimes by a mud-pillar shrine of Kala Pir, where the Yogis, who are another misty division of holy men, would receive him as they do those who know what castes and divisions are worth; sometimes on the outskirts of a little Hindu village, where the children would steal up with the food their parents had prepared; and sometimes on the pitch of the bare grazing-grounds, where the flame of his stick fire waked the drowsy camels. It was all one to Purun Dass – or Purun Bhagat, as he called himself now. Earth, people, and food were all one. But unconsciously his feet drew him away northward and eastward; from the south to Rohtak; from Rohtak to Kurnool; from Kurnool to ruined Samanah, and then up-stream along the dried bed of the Gugger river that fills only when the rain falls in the hills, till one day he saw the far line of the great Himalayas.

Then Purun Bhagat smiled, for he remembered that his mother was of Rajput Brahmin birth, from Kulu way – a Hill-woman, always home-sick for the snows – and that the least touch of Hill blood draws a man in the end back to where he belongs.

"Yonder," said Purun Bhagat, breasting the lower slopes of the Sewaliks, where the cacti stand up like seven-branched candle-sticks-"yonder I shall sit down and get knowledge"; and the cool wind of the Himalayas whistled about his ears as he trod the road that led to Simla.

The last time he had come that way it had been in state, with a clattering cavalry escort, to visit the gentlest and most affable of Viceroys; and the two had talked for an hour together about mutual friends in London, and what the Indian common folk really thought of things. This time Purun Bhagat paid no calls, but leaned on the rail of the Mall, watching that glorious view of the Plains spread out forty miles below, till a native Mohammedan policeman told him he was obstructing traffic; and Purun Bhagat salaamed reverently to the Law, because he knew the value of it, and was seeking for a Law of his own. Then he moved on, and slept that night in an empty hut at Chota Simla, which looks like the very last end of the earth, but it was only the beginning of his journey. He followed the Himalaya–Thibet road, the little ten-foot track that is blasted out of solid rock, or strutted out on timbers over gulfs a thousand feet deep; that dips into warm, wet, shut-in valleys, and climbs out across bare, grassy hill-shoulders where the sun strikes like a burning-glass; or turns through dripping, dark forests where the tree-ferns dress the trunks from head to heel, and the pheasant calls to his mate. And he met Thibetan herdsmen with their dogs and flocks of sheep, each sheep with a little bag of borax on his back, and wandering wood-cutters, and cloaked and blanketed Lamas from Thibet, coming into India on pilgrimage, and envoys of little solitary Hill-states, posting furiously on ring-streaked and piebald ponies, or the cavalcade of a Rajah paying a visit; or else for a long, clear day he would see nothing more than a black bear grunting and rooting below in the valley. When he first started, the roar of the world he had left still rang in his ears, as the roar of a tunnel rings long after the train has passed through; but when he had put the Mutteeanee Pass behind him that was all done, and Purun Bhagat was alone with himself, walking, wondering, and thinking, his eyes on the ground, and his thoughts with the clouds.

One evening he crossed the highest pass he had met till then – it had been a two-day's climb – and came out on a line of snow-peaks that banded all the horizon – mountains from fifteen to twenty thousand feet high, looking almost near enough to hit with a stone, though they were fifty or sixty miles away. The pass was crowned with dense, dark forest – deodar, walnut, wild cherry, wild olive, and wild pear, but mostly deodar, which is the Himalayan cedar; and under the shadow of the deodars stood a deserted shrine to Kali – who is Durga, who is Sitala, who is sometimes worshipped against the smallpox.

Purun Dass swept the stone floor clean, smiled at the grinning statue, made himself a little mud fireplace at the back of the shrine, spread his antelope skin on a bed of fresh pine-needles, tucked his bairagi – his brass-handled crutch – under his armpit, and sat down to rest.

Immediately below him the hillside fell away, clean and cleared for fifteen hundred feet, where a little village of stone-walled houses, with roofs of beaten earth, clung to the steep tilt. All round it the tiny terraced fields lay out like aprons of patchwork on the knees of the mountain, and cows no bigger than beetles grazed between the smooth stone circles of the threshing-floors. Looking across the valley, the eye was deceived by the size of things, and could not at first realise that what seemed to be low scrub, on the opposite mountain-flank, was in truth a forest of hundred-foot pines. Purun Bhagat saw an eagle swoop across the gigantic hollow, but the great bird dwindled to a dot ere it was half-way over. A few bands of scattered clouds strung up and down the valley, catching on a shoulder of the hills, or rising up and dying out when they were level with the head of the pass. And "Here shall I find peace," said Purun Bhagat.

Now, a Hill-man makes nothing of a few hundred feet up or down, and as soon as the villagers saw the smoke in the deserted shrine, the village priest climbed up the terraced hillside to welcome the stranger.

When he met Purun Bhagat's eyes – the eyes of a man used to control thousands – he bowed to the earth, took the begging-bowl without a word, and returned to the village, saying, "We have at last a holy man. Never have I seen such a man. He is of the Plains – but pale-coloured – a Brahmin of the Brahmins." Then all the housewives of the village said, "Think you he will stay with us?" and each did her best to cook the most savoury meal for the Bhagat. Hill-food is very simple, but with buckwheat and Indian corn, and rice and red pepper, and little fish out of the stream in the valley, and honey from the flue-like hives built in the stone walls, and dried apricots, and turmeric, and wild ginger, and bannocks of flour, a devout woman can make good things, and it was a full bowl that the priest carried to the Bhagat. Was he going to stay? asked the priest. Would he need a chela – a disciple – to beg for him? Had he a blanket against the cold weather? Was the food good?

Purun Bhagat ate, and thanked the giver. It was in his mind to stay. That was sufficient, said the priest. Let the begging-bowl be placed outside the shrine, in the hollow made by those two twisted roots, and daily should the Bhagat be fed; for the village felt honoured that such a man – he looked timidly into the Bhagat's face – should tarry among them.

That day saw the end of Purun Bhagat's wanderings. He had come to the place appointed for him – the silence and the space. After this, time stopped, and he, sitting at the mouth of the shrine, could not tell whether he were alive or dead; a man with control of his limbs, or a part of the hills, and the clouds, and the shifting rain and sunlight. He would repeat a Name softly to himself a hundred hundred times, till, at each repetition, he seemed to move more and more out of his body, sweeping up to the doors of some tremendous discovery; but, just as the door was opening, his body would drag him back, and, with grief, he felt he was locked up again in the flesh and bones of Purun Bhagat.

Every morning the filled begging-bowl was laid silently in the crutch of the roots outside the shrine. Sometimes the priest brought it; sometimes a Ladakhi trader, lodging in the village, and anxious to get merit, trudged up the path; but, more often, it was the woman who had cooked the meal overnight; and she would murmur, hardly above her breath. "Speak for me before the gods, Bhagat. Speak for such a one, the wife of so-and-so!" Now and then some bold child would be allowed the honour, and Purun Bhagat would hear him drop the bowl and run as fast as his little legs could carry him, but the Bhagat never came down to the village. It was laid out like a map at his feet. He could see the evening gatherings, held on the circle of the threshing-floors, because that was the only level ground; could see the wonderful unnamed green of the young rice, the indigo blues of the Indian corn, the dock-like patches of buckwheat, and, in its season, the red bloom of the amaranth, whose tiny seeds, being neither grain nor pulse, make a food that can be lawfully eaten by Hindus in time of fasts.

When the year turned, the roofs of the huts were all little squares of purest gold, for it was on the roofs that they laid out their cobs of the corn to dry. Hiving and harvest, rice-sowing and husking, passed before his eyes, all embroidered down there on the many-sided plots of fields, and he thought of them all, and wondered what they all led to at the long last.

Even in populated India a man cannot a day sit still before the wild things run over him as though he were a rock; and in that wilderness very soon the wild things, who knew Kali's Shrine well, came back to look at the intruder. The *langurs*, the big gray-whiskered monkeys of the Himalayas, were, naturally, the first, for they are alive with curiosity; and when they had upset the begging-bowl, and rolled it round the floor, and tried their teeth on the brass-handled crutch, and made faces at the antelope skin, they decided that the human being who sat so still was harmless. At evening, they would leap down from the pines, and beg with their hands for things to eat, and then swing off in graceful curves. They liked the warmth of the fire, too, and huddled round it till Purun Bhagat had to push them aside to throw on more fuel; and in the morning, as often as not, he would find a furry ape sharing his blanket. All day long, one or other of the tribe would sit by his side, staring out at the snows, crooning and looking unspeakably wise and sorrowful.

After the monkeys came the *barasingh*, that big deer which is like our red deer, but stronger. He wished to rub off the velvet of his horns against the cold stones of Kali's statue, and stamped his feet when he saw the man at the shrine. But Purun Bhagat never moved, and, little by little, the royal stag edged up and nuzzled his shoulder. Purun Bhagat slid one cool hand along the hot antlers, and the touch soothed the fretted beast, who bowed his head, and Purun Bhagat very softly rubbed and ravelled off the velvet. Afterward, the barasingh brought his doe and fawn – gentle things that mumbled on the holy man's blanket – or would come alone at night, his eyes green in the fire-flicker, to take his share of fresh walnuts. At last, the musk-deer, the shyest and almost the smallest of the deerlets, came, too, her big rabbity ears erect; even brindled, silent *mushick-nabha* must needs find out what the light in the shrine meant, and drop out her moose-like nose into Purun Bhagat's lap, coming and going with the shadows of the fire. Purun Bhagat called them all 'my brothers,' and his low call of *'Bhai! Bhai!'* would draw them from the forest at noon if they were within ear shot. The Himalayan black bear, moody and suspicious – Sona, who has the V-shaped white mark under his chin – passed that way more than once; and since the Bhagat showed no fear, Sona showed no anger, but watched him, and came closer, and begged a share of the caresses, and a dole of bread or wild berries. Often, in the still dawns, when the Bhagat would climb to the very crest of the pass to watch the red day walking along the peaks of the snows, he would find Sona shuffling and grunting at his heels, thrusting, a curious fore-paw under fallen trunks, and bringing it away with a WHOOF of impatience; or his early steps would wake Sona where he lay curled up, and the great brute, rising erect, would think to fight, till he heard the Bhagat's voice and knew his best friend.

Nearly all hermits and holy men who live apart from the big cities have the reputation of being able to work miracles with the wild things, but all the miracle lies in keeping still, in never making a hasty movement, and, for a long time, at least, in never looking directly at a visitor. The villagers saw the outline of the *barasingh* stalking like a shadow through the dark forest behind the shrine; saw the *minaul*, the Himalayan pheasant, blazing in her best colours before Kali's statue; and the *langurs* on their haunches, inside, playing with the walnut shells. Some of the children, too, had heard Sona singing to himself, bear-fashion, behind the fallen rocks, and the Bhagat's reputation as miracle-worker stood firm.

Yet nothing was farther from his mind than miracles. He believed that all things were one big Miracle, and when a man knows that much he knows something to go upon. He knew for a certainty that there was nothing great and nothing little in this world: and day and night he strove to think out his way into the heart of things, back to the place whence his soul had come.

So thinking, his untrimmed hair fell down about his shoulders, the stone slab at the side of the antelope skin was dented into a little hole by the foot of his brass-handled crutch, and the place between the tree-trunks, where the begging-bowl rested day after day, sunk and wore into a hollow almost as smooth as the brown shell itself; and each beast knew his exact place at the fire. The fields changed their colours with the seasons; the threshing-floors filled and emptied, and filled again and again; and again and again, when winter came, the *langurs* frisked among the branches feathered with light snow, till the mother-monkeys brought their sad-eyed little babies up from the warmer valleys with the spring. There were few changes in the village. The priest was older, and many of the little children who used to come with the begging-dish sent their own children now; and when you asked of the villagers how long their holy man had lived in Kali's Shrine at the head of the pass, they answered, 'Always.'

Then came such summer rains as had not been known in the Hills for many seasons. Through three good months the valley was wrapped in cloud and soaking mist – steady, unrelenting downfall, breaking off into thunder-shower after thunder-shower.

Kali's Shrine stood above the clouds, for the most part, and there was a whole month in which the Bhagat never caught a glimpse of his village. It was packed away under a white floor of cloud that swayed and shifted and rolled on itself and bulged upward, but never broke from its piers – the streaming flanks of the valley.

All that time he heard nothing but the sound of a million little waters, overhead from the trees, and underfoot along the ground, soaking through the pine-needles, dripping from the tongues of draggled fern, and spouting in newly-torn muddy channels down the slopes. Then the sun came out, and drew forth the good incense of the deodars and the rhododendrons, and that far-off, clean smell which the Hill people call 'the smell of the snows.' The hot sunshine lasted for a week, and then the rains gathered together for their last downpour, and the water fell in sheets that flayed off the skin of the ground and leaped back in mud. Purun Bhagat heaped his fire high that night, for he was sure his brothers would need warmth; but never a beast came to the shrine, though he called and called till he dropped asleep, wondering what had happened in the woods.

It was in the black heart of the night, the rain drumming like a thousand drums, that he was roused by a plucking at his blanket, and, stretching out, felt the little hand of a *langur*. 'It is better here than in the trees,' he said sleepily, loosening a fold of blanket; 'take it and be warm.' The monkey caught his hand and pulled hard. 'Is it food, then?' said Purun Bhagat. 'Wait awhile, and I will prepare some.' As he kneeled to throw fuel on the fire the *langur* ran to the door of the shrine, crooned and ran back again, plucking at the man's knee.

'What is it? What is thy trouble, Brother?' said Purun Bhagat, for the *langur*'s eyes were full of things that he could not tell. 'Unless one of thy caste be in a trap – and none set traps here – I will not go into that weather. Look, Brother, even the *barasingh* comes for shelter!'

The deer's antlers clashed as he strode into the shrine, clashed against the grinning statue of Kali. He lowered them in Purun Bhagat's direction and stamped uneasily, hissing through his half-shut nostrils.

'Hai! Hai! Hai!' said the Bhagat, snapping his fingers, 'Is THIS payment for a night's lodging?' But the deer pushed him toward the door, and as he did so Purun Bhagat heard the sound of something opening with a sigh, and saw two slabs of the floor draw away from each other, while the sticky earth below smacked its lips.

'Now I see,' said Purun Bhagat. 'No blame to my brothers that they did not sit by the fire to-night. The mountain is falling. And yet – why should I go?' His eye fell on the empty begging-bowl, and his face changed. 'They have given me good food daily since – since I came, and, if I am not swift, tomorrow there will not be one mouth in the valley. Indeed, I must go and warn them below. Back there, Brother! Let me get to the fire.'

The *barasingh* backed unwillingly as Purun Bhagat drove a pine torch deep into the flame, twirling it till it was well lit. 'Ah! ye came to warn me,' he said, rising. 'Better than that we shall do; better than that. Out, now, and lend me thy neck, Brother, for I have but two feet.'

He clutched the bristling withers of the *barasingh* with his right hand, held the torch away with his left, and stepped out of the shrine into the desperate night. There was no breath of wind, but the rain nearly drowned the flare as the great deer hurried down the slope, sliding on his haunches. As soon as they were clear of the forest more of the Bhagat's brothers joined them. He heard, though he could not see, the *langurs* pressing about him, and behind them the uhh! uhh! of Sona. The rain matted his long white hair into ropes; the water splashed beneath his bare feet, and his yellow robe clung to his frail old body, but he stepped down steadily, leaning against the *barasingh*. He was no longer a holy man, but Sir Purun Dass, K.C.I.E., Prime Minister of no small State, a man accustomed to command, going out to save life. Down the steep, plashy path they poured all together, the Bhagat and his brothers, down and down till the deer's feet clicked and stumbled on the wall of a threshing-floor, and he snorted because he smelt Man. Now they were at the head of the one crooked village street, and the Bhagat beat with his crutch on the barred windows of the blacksmith's house, as his torch blazed up in the shelter of the eaves. 'Up and out!' cried Purun Bhagat; and he did not know his own voice, for it was years since he had spoken aloud to a man. 'The hill falls! The hill is falling! Up and out, oh, you within!'

"It is our Bhagat," said the blacksmith's wife. 'He stands among his beasts. Gather the little ones and give the call.'

It ran from house to house, while the beasts, cramped in the narrow way, surged and huddled round the Bhagat, and Sona puffed impatiently.

The people hurried into the street – they were no more than seventy souls all told – and in the glare of the torches they saw their Bhagat holding back the terrified *barasingh*, while the monkeys plucked piteously at his skirts, and Sona sat on his haunches and roared.

'Across the valley and up the next hill!' shouted Purun Bhagat. 'Leave none behind! We follow!'

Then the people ran as only Hill folk can run, for they knew that in a landslip you must climb for the highest ground across the valley. They fled, splashing through the little river at the bottom, and panted up the terraced fields on the far side, while the Bhagat and his brethren followed. Up and up the opposite mountain they climbed, calling to each other by name – the roll-call of the village – and at their heels toiled the big *barasingh*, weighted by the failing strength of Purun Bhagat. At last the deer stopped in the shadow of a deep pinewood, five hundred feet up the hillside. His instinct, that had warned him of the coming slide, told him he would he safe here.

Purun Bhagat dropped fainting by his side, for the chill of the rain and that fierce climb were killing him; but first he called to the scattered torches ahead, 'Stay and count your numbers'; then, whispering to the deer as he saw the lights gather in a cluster: 'Stay with me, Brother. Stay – till – I– go!'

There was a sigh in the air that grew to a mutter, and a mutter that grew to a roar, and a roar that passed all sense of hearing, and the hillside on which the villagers stood was hit in the darkness, and rocked to the blow. Then a note as steady, deep, and true as the deep C of the organ drowned everything for perhaps five minutes, while the very roots of the pines quivered to it. It died away, and the sound of the rain falling on miles of hard ground and grass changed to the muffled drum of water on soft earth. That told its own tale.

Never a villager – not even the priest – was bold enough to speak to the Bhagat who had saved their lives. They crouched under the pines and waited till the day. When it came they looked across the valley and saw that what had been forest, and terraced field, and track-threaded grazing-ground was one raw, red, fan-shaped smear, with a few trees flung head-down on the scarp. That red ran high up the hill of their refuge, damming back the little river, which had begun to spread into a brick-coloured lake. Of the village, of the road to the shrine, of the shrine itself, and the forest behind, there was no trace. For one mile in width and two thousand feet in sheer depth the mountain-side had come away bodily, planed clean from head to heel.

And the villagers, one by one, crept through the wood to pray before their Bhagat. They saw the *barasingh* standing over him, who fled when they came near, and they heard the *langurs* wailing in the branches, and Sona moaning up the hill; but their Bhagat was dead, sitting cross-legged, his back against a tree, his crutch under his armpit, and his face turned to the north-east.

The priest said: 'Behold a miracle after a miracle, for in this very attitude must all Sunnyasis be buried! Therefore where he now is we will build the temple to our holy man.'

They built the temple before a year was ended – a little stone-and-earth shrine – and they called the hill the Bhagat's hill, and they worship there with lights and flowers and offerings to this day. But they do not know that the saint of their worship is the late Sir Purun Dass, K.C.I.E., D.C.L., Ph.D., etc., once Prime Minister of the progressive and enlightened State of Mohiniwala, and honorary or corresponding member of more learned and scientific societies than will ever do any good in this world or the next.

BUCK'S QUIZ

BODY PARTS

Angela Macmillan

1. Which novel is set in The Republic of Gilead, a theocratic military dictatorship formed in a future North America after the government of the USA has been overthrown?
2. A teenage girl, after being raped and murdered, watches her family from heaven as they grieve and try to come to terms with the circumstances of her death. What is her name?
3. The film, *Apocalypse Now*, is based on which novel?
4. The last line of Stephen Vincent Benet's poem which begins 'I have fallen in love with American names' , is the title of which famous history book published in 1970?
5. Whose 'vast and trunkless legs' 'stand in the desert'?
6. Catherine Barkley, an English nurse, dies at the end of which 1929 novel?
7. Amity, a fictional seaside resort on Long Island is the setting for which novel?
8. Who advises a blind man: 'A man may see how this world goes with no eyes. Look with thine ears'?
9. Archie Jones, an Englishman and Samad Iqbal, a Bengali Muslim, are best friends in which prize-winning novel?
10. Which short story concerns two men minding sheep in Wyoming?
11. Susan Trinder and Maud Lilly are the narrators of which historical crime novel?
12. 'And the azurous hung hills are his world-wielding shoulder/ Majestic – as a stallion stalwart, very-violet-sweet.' What time of year is the poet describing?

Cassandra   No.55

ACROSS

7. Unspecified person however wayward. (7)
8. Died of a sore throat? (7)
10. Dancing ladies provide perfect examples (6)
11. Reckless ambassador joins journalist on the French ship (8)
12. Juno's other identity in her active role as sister and wife (4)
13. Proposition of compliance (10)
14. Try new scout movement in the region (4, 7)
19. Turbulent weather in north for someone with final chance (4, 6)
22. Narrative provided by a mortal enemy (4)
23. An event I arranged might include Bassanio for example (8)
24. Daniel, confused is caught out in a lie (6)
25. Conciliation service infiltrated by intelligence agency in the shrubbery (7)
26. Fashionable young ladies wandering alone inside ship (7)

DOWN

*1 & 18 down. The main alternative to the devil (3, 4, 4, 3)
* 2 & 5 down. Break up schedules for dining arrangements (8, 5)
3. Animals beginning to browse eagerly and starting to smell (6)
4. Milk supplier originally from Holland (8)
* **5.** See 2 down
* **6.** See 9 down
* **9 & 6 down.** Poetic translation of Aeschylus? (3, 8, 7)
15. Calypso's home, usually twinned with Bogota mistakenly (8)
* **16.** See 17 down
* **17 & 16 down.** Playwright is moving target in a centre (7,8)
* **18.** See 1 down
20. Where Tommy Atkins often found refuge (6)
21. In part pulling rank led to cause of resentment (6)

*Clues with an asterisk have a common theme

PRIZES

The winner of the Crossword (plucked in time-honoured tradition from a hat) will receive a book prize courtesy of Vintage Classics, and the same to the winner of the fiendishly difficult Buck's Quiz.

Congratulations to Steve Bowkett, Cardiff and to Sarah Wright (Tyne and Wear) for soundly beating Buck at her Quiz; and to Steve Bowkett who also wins the Crossword prize. Well done on doing the Double, Steve!

Please send your solutions (marked Cassandra Crossword or Buck's Quiz) to The Reader, Calderstones Mansion House, Calderstones Park, Liverpool, L18 3JB. The deadline for answers is 28 October.

ANSWERS

CASSANDRA CROSSWORD NO. 54

Across

8. Diminish **9.** Animal **10.** Dear **11.** Pirandello **12.** George **14.** Aviators **15.** Unclear **17.** Cyanide **20.** Costello **22.** Enigma **23.** Swivelling **24.** Four **25.** Glutei **26.** Alter ego

Down

1. Nineteen **2.** Pier **3.** Dimple **4.** The road **5.** Jauntily **6.** Dilettanti **7.** Gaoler **13.** Relativity **16.** Alleluia **18.** Demiurge **16.** Abyss **19.** To Wigan **21.** Orwell **22.** Eighty **24.** Farm

BUCK'S QUIZ NO. 61

1. 'Summer's lease' Sonnet 18, Shakespeare **2.** *The Summer Book,* Tove Jansson **3.** *Suddenly Last Summer,* Tennessee Williams **4.** *Summer Crossing,* Truman Capote **5.** 'Bredon Hill', A.E.Housman **6.** *In a Summer Season,* Elizabeth Taylor **7.** 'The Last Rose of Summer', Thomas Moore **8.** 'In summer, quite the other way / I have to go to bed by day', R.L.Stevenson **9.** 'The Nightingale', John Keats **10.** 'The Cuckoo Song' **11.** *Summer,* Edith Wharton **12.** *The Go-Between,* L.P.Hartley

CONTRIBUTORS

Nick Benefield is a psychotherapist and policy maker. Nick was Department of Health Personality Disorder Advisor and Joint DoH/NOMS (National Offender Management Service) Offender PD Programme Head. Recently retired, he lives with his wife, Jen, in Cheshire.

Jane Bonnyman is from Edinburgh and studied English at the University of St Andrews before completing her teaching diploma. Her poems have appeared in *Caterpillar Children's Magazine*, *Poetry Salzburg Review* and *Gutter*. Currently she writes poetry resources for the BBC and is working on other literary projects.

David Constantine's most recent volume of poems is *Elder*, 2014 (Bloodaxe Books). 2015 saw the publication of *In Another Country: Selected Stories* and his novel *The Life-Writer* (both Comma Press). The 2015 film *45 Years* starring Tom Courtney and Charlotte Rampling, is based on his short story 'In Another Country', first published in *The Reader*, issue 9.

Gareth Culshaw lives in Wales, and hopes one day to achieve something special with the pen. He finds his inspiration from the great outdoors. His website is Gculshaw.co.uk

Kim Devereux is the author of *Rembrandt's Mirror,* a debut novel selected for WHSmith Travel's Fresh Talent promotion, showcasing the best in new and emerging authors and long-listed for the prestigious 2016 HWA Goldsboro Debut Crown Award).

Angelina D'Roza is poet in residence at Bank Street Arts and writing mentor with the Koestler Trust. Her work includes collaborations with visual artists and sound artists, and her poems have appeared in a range of publications. Her first collection, *Envies the Birds*, was published by Longbarrow Press (March 2016).

Grace Farrington is Quality Practice Assistant at The Reader.

Jennie Feldman, a freelance writer and translator, has published two poetry collections, *The Lost Notebook* (2005) and *Swift* (2012). She has translated work by Jacques Réda and is co-author, with Stephen Romer, of *Into the Deep Street: Seven Modern French Poets, 1938–2008* (2009), which was shortlisted for the Popescu Prize. She lives in Jerusalem and Oxford.

Conor McCormack is a Bristol-based filmmaker, writer and psychoanalyst. For three years he has documented the Bristol Hearing Voices Network – a self-help group for people who hear voices and have other unusual experiences.

Ian McMillan was born in 1956 and has been a freelance writer/performer /broadcaster since 1981. He presents *The Verb* on BBC Radio 3 every Friday night.

Alexis McNay is a former project worker and remains a friend of The Reader.

Bibhu Padhi born Bibhu Prasad Padhi, is an Indian poet and writer. He writes in English and Oriya languages. He is also a literary critic and translator.

Vincent Parker lives in Widnes and works as an engineer throughout the UK. Poems published in several magazines including Rialto, *North*, *Smoke*, *Planet*, *Magma*.

Stuart Pickford lives in Harrogate where he teaches in a local school. He is married with three children.

Enid Stubin is Associate Professor of English at Kingsborough Community College of the City University of New York and Adjunct Professor of Humanities at NY University's School of Continuing and Professional Studies.

Distribution Information

Trade orders Contact Mark Chilver, Magazine Department, Central Books

> email: mark@centralbooks.com
> web: www.centralbooks.com
> tel: 0845 458 9925   fax: 0845 458 9912
> Central Books, 99 Wallis Road, London, E9 5LN

All other queries regarding trade orders or institutional subscriptions
Contact The Reader Office

> email: magazine@thereader.org.uk
> tel: 0151 729 2200

SUBSCRIBE

£18 per year with Direct Debit

Print off an order form from our website (www.thereader.org.uk), call us on 0151 729 2200 or email (magazine@thereader.org.uk) and we will send you a form in the post.

Cost by Cheque or PayPal:

UK Subscription: four issues for £24 (inc. p&p)
Abroad Subscription: four issues for £36 (inc. p&p)

Please make cheques payable to The Reader and post to: The Reader, FREEPOST RSSL-UHCB-EKKE, Calderstones Mansion House, Calderstones Park, Liverpool, L18 3JB.

Don't forget to include your name and address, and the issue number with which you would like your subscription to begin.

The cheapest payment method for overseas readers is by PayPal via our website: www.thereader.org.uk

Please direct email enquiries to:
subscriptions@thereader.org.uk

the reader